THE DAY BEFORE TOMORROW

HOW TO MAKE TODAY COUNT!

MADISON N. NGAFEESON, PHD

The Day Before Tomorrow: How to Make Today Count!
Trilogy Christian Publishers A Wholly Owned Subsidiary of Trinity
Broadcasting Network
2442 Michelle Drive Tustin, CA 92780
Rights Department, 2442 Michelle Drive, Tustin, CA 92780.
Trilogy Christian Publishing/TBN and colophon are trademarks of Trinity
Broadcasting Network.
Cover design by: Kelly Stewart
For information about special discounts for bulk purchases, please contact
Trilogy Christian Publishing.
Trilogy Disclaimer: The views and content expressed in this book are those
of the author and may not necessarily reflect the views and doctrine of
Trilogy Christian Publishing or the Trinity Broadcasting Network.
Manufactured in the United States of America
10 9 8 7 6 5 4 3 2 1
Library of Congress Cataloging-in-Publication Data is available.
ISBN: 979-8-88738-196-1
E-ISBN: 979-8-88738-197-8

PRAISE REVIEWS

"An insightful read. We must understand yesterday so we can live tomorrow today!"

–Yaah Gladys Shang Viban
Inspirational Speaker, LEAD Missions International

"'The Day Before Tomorrow' brilliantly exposes the many ways in which we can live our lives to the fullest today. It beautifully combines engaging motivational storytelling with guided journaling."

–Michelle Salinas
Journalist and Professional Public Speaker

"...one of the most insightful books today when it comes to living every day to the fullest and with the future in mind. Expertly written and authentically revealing..."

–Frankie Powell
Providence LEAD

"...An intriguing page-turner of monumental proportions written for a 21st-century audience."

–Reverend Jesse Song
Author, Ministry Consultant, Royal City Mission, London

"...A book that breathes hope to the hopeless, vision to the blind, and courage to the dreamer to know that it's not over as long as there is a today."

–Eyong Enoh
Football Coach, Author, Podcast Host, and CEO (4pballer)

"You will close this book inspired to live the rest of your life with the desire to leave a legacy for humanity!"

–Cathy Garcia
Certified Speaker & Executive Pastor

"An eye-opener. I recommend this work to anyone who wants more than what is obtainable in their life presently."

–Professor Victor Mbarika
President, Board of Trustees, The ICT University

TABLE OF CONTENTS

DEDICATION

This book is dedicated to two important sets of influencers in my life. First, my family, namely, my wife, Claudia; our three lovely children, Triumph, Lamb, and Madison (Jr.); and my late grandparents, Mr. Simon and Mrs. Rebecca Ngafeeson. You all have taught me practical ways on how to make today count as a husband, father, professional, and leader. Your positive influence on my perspective on *today* is undeniable.

Last but certainly not least, I dedicate this book to *you* who, like me, is thirsty and hungry for significance and won't settle for less. You, who have refused to be trapped in yesterday or fooled by empty desires of tomorrow and are daily obsessed with living in the *now*! This book is for you.

ACKNOWLEDGMENTS

This book would have been impossible without the contributions of some of the biggest friends in my life, whose stories I have also featured along with mine. I want to thank my dear friends Kevin Taylor, Eliud Garcia, and Cathy Garcia. Kevin's life-altering story is featured in the early parts of this book, while Eliud and Cathy's daring leadership story is featured in the concluding chapters. Thank you for adding color to this work by permitting me to share your stories.

I'd also like to thank my writing team. You were generous with your ideas, insights, corrections, and edits that have made this work stand out. Thank you, Alicia Dale, Amanda Ayers Barnet, and Metta Såma. Time will fail me to mention all the project managers and the publication team. I am indebted to you for the quality of this project.

Finally, I want to thank all my mentors and mentees over the years, whom I cannot name all here. Thank you, Dr. Julius Esunge, Dr. Myles Munroe, Dr. John C. Maxwell, and Mr. Frankie Powell, for your mentorship. The wisdom I have gleaned from you all has helped me become all that I am today. A big "thank you" to all my mentees who have provided me over the past twenty-five years with the opportunity to try the principles and learn the lessons that I now share with you in this book. Thank you for being forgiving of me when I made mistakes. You all made leadership come alive to me.

FOREWORD

I'd met Madison *at* Harvard University a year earlier.
I emphasize "at" since all our classes were on Zoom due
to the COVID-19 pandemic. When I heard Madison and his
family were coming to Southern California for vacation,
I could not wait to see what he looked like in 3D. Up until
then, Madison's entire existence was restricted to one of
forty-five little boxes on my screen. He sat in his little chair
at his little desk in his little office in his little square. Now,
here *I* was sitting outside his life-sized hotel, staring at the
life-sized ocean, grateful for my good luck at being in this
incredible spot on such a glorious day...

"Kelly, my friend!"

I felt his powerful voice and thundering laugh far more
than I heard it. I jumped up from my bench, spun around,
and found myself face to (3D) face with the very real Dr.
Madison Ngafeeson. We skipped the handshake and went
directly in for the embrace.

Madison, it turns out, is a *formidable* human being—in
both size and spirit. The amount of energy that poured
into me through that hug completely overshadowed the
fact that he was squeezing the life out of me. If I were in a
video game, Madison would have just powered me up. It
would have been one thing to only feel that level of energy

in our first meeting, but it happens *every single time* I am in his presence.

And *that*, my dear readers, is the point.

That is Madison's superpower!

The ability to maintain and exude this constant, unflagging energy is an extraordinary superpower. Mighty. Relentless. A bottomless well of gratitude, positivity, and generosity. To sustain this superpower in a normal person would take the energy of a nuclear reactor and probably burn them out. But in Madison, I am convinced, it is part of his DNA, and it nourishes him as much as it nourishes everybody he touches.

And now, after reading *The Day After Tomorrow—Dr. Madison's Secret Exposed!*—my own made up title—I understand where this energy comes from. Madison truly, unequivocally, unapologetically lives in the moment.

Upon experiencing *The Day After Tomorrow: How to Make Today Count*, I was reminded of two consequential moments in my life that illustrate the teachings found in this book. We all have these revelatory events that make us stop and think and then readjust our worldview. Often, we are so caught up in our day-to-day that we don't honor how much these moments shape us until we are nudged into rekindling those revelations. Experiencing Madison's wisdom in the book brought mine up for me again and reminded me of just how much the events I am sharing have helped *me* put my "Yesterdays" and "Tomorrows" in their appropriate context, allowing me to focus on my present—my "Today"—and how important it is to embrace it.

Several years ago, I was asked to preside over a wedding of a couple in their mid-to-late thirties. I am requested to officiate nuptials from time to time, which never ceases to amaze and humble me. My strategy in ministering to these weddings is to dig deep into couples' lives and create an inspirational message that reflects their journey to the altar. This couple's story was—at least in my experience— unique. Of course, they had wonderfully positive events throughout each of their lives. The challenges, however, were equally heartbreaking and inspirational. Both struggled with addiction, and during those periods, they disappointed friends, their families, and most importantly themselves. Their struggles were so difficult that most of us would have simply given up, yet something caused them to persist. By their wedding day, they were both celebrating several years of sobriety.

When I heard this amazing story of challenge, despair, strength, and redemption, I had an overwhelming feeling of just how miraculous this moment was. Had tßhey not gone through these unthinkable trials and tribulations, they never would have crossed each other's paths. Everything they went through separately resulted in their chance meeting. And now they were standing at the altar together. I asked them, "If it meant giving up this moment, what in your past would you change?" Their answer was, "Not a single thing!"

I have often reflected on that moment since. If the path they took got them to that altar on that day, then we must look at their every step as a blessing! Every challenge and every stumble—which at the time felt horribly unfair and devastating—pointed them to the perfection of the moment.

The lesson? If we have even the slightest regret over our yesterday, then we are denying the gift of today.

The second of my life lessons happened in 2016 while visiting my eldest son in Sydney, Australia. With one son in San Francisco, one in Australia, and my wife Carla and I living in Los Angeles, getting the family together can be a daunting task. In one of those unique moments, we were all in Sydney at the same time. We had just finished an amazing meal and said goodnight to my eldest; my wife, Carla, our youngest son, and I were walking back to our hotel. It was an amazing evening. We laughed through the entire meal. Our gratitude for being together as a family again could not have been higher. We continued joking and laughing as we crossed the street. Then, as we got to the middle of the road, I felt like I'd been hit by a bolt of lightning. A blood clot lodged itself in my brain. I immediately felt dizzy and asked my son to assist me to the sidewalk. I remember a panicked Carla telling me to "Move your hands, speak to me, look at me, stay awake!" I remember thinking that all I really needed was to lie down on that sidewalk and sleep. I was slipping.

After three days in the hospital and a few months more of recovery, I was jarred by the realization that my life could have ended on that street in Sydney. One moment, I was enjoying the absolute best time of my life, and in an instant, I was fighting for it. I know what you are thinking.

The obvious lesson is that we should appreciate today since we cannot count on tomorrow. That was not *my* lesson.

The moment before I had that stroke, I was *alive!* I was *laughing!* I was experiencing *true joy!* I am eternally grateful that I survived to live another day, but that is not really the point. I understand now that tomorrow cannot be guaranteed, but that, too, is not the point. We are all, without question, going to pass over to the other side someday. We have no idea when or how, but all our lives end.

The point is: When that time comes, were we living in the moment? Were we experiencing the unbridled joy offered by the miracle of the moment? I continue to reflect, not on the stroke, but on the incredible, exciting, loving instant just before. *That* is the point.

And that is Madison's superpower. He lives for Today. Sure, he *plans* for tomorrow, but he is not willing to *wait* for tomorrow. Then he strings all these amazing "Todays" together to create a lifetime of overwhelming positive energy—the energy that filled me the first time we met and continues to do so every time I see him.

The Day Before Tomorrow: How to Make Today Count is *your* roadmap, not to the future, but to today. Enjoy the trip!

Kelly Kimball
Tech Entrepreneur, Philanthropist, Lecturer,
Founder & Board Chairman (VITU)

PREFACE

In March of 2017, I was attending my first International Maxwell Certification event in Orlando, Florida. I had awoken to a great spring day I will never forget. It was a day filled with hope and anticipation of all that lay before me. The *New York Times* best-selling author, leadership guru, and world-renowned speaker John C. Maxwell would be presenting along with many other impressive leaders. I was passionate about growing my speaking, coaching, and leadership skills. In fact, I was elated that later that morning, I would be listening to my favorite leadership mentor of all times, Mr. John C. Maxwell.

Speaker after speaker took the podium. The energy in the room began to shift. The electricity could be felt as the time drew near for Mr. Maxwell to address the eager participants. The master of ceremonies had barely finished her introduction before the room of over 2,500 attendees exploded with applause and a standing ovation to greet Mr. Maxwell as he approached the podium.

Mr. Maxwell spoke eloquently in a heart-to-heart presentation to the audience. In his usual friendly and affectionate tone, his kind and caring words embraced the crowd. As expected, he gave a great presentation that wowed me and left me deeply pensive: *What if, after all, I could become the man I have always dreamed of? What if I could truly be a man who added value to everyone I met? What if I spent the rest of my life accomplishing my desire to create change in the world? What if it was doable, after all? What if I started today and now?*

A slew of questions was dashing through my mind.

Before I had time to thoroughly process these thoughts, Mr. Maxwell paused and started talking about a book he wanted us to get for ourselves and our loved ones.

"I want you to get this book," he said. "It is a special book. It's so special; I wrote a note for you in my handwriting and with my signature."

This last statement got my attention.

Then he added, "The book is entitled *The Greatest Story Ever Told.*"

At this point, my mind began to race.

"What could this story be about? Who is the main character in this story?" I wondered. "Maybe George Washington, or Teddy Roosevelt, or Thomas Edison, or Harriet Tubman, or Martin Luther King, or Nelson Mandela, or Mahatma Gandhi, or Mother Teresa, or a combination of some of these great men and women?"

I think it must be Jesus Christ! I thought to myself. After all, he's the biggest larger-than-life figure of all time!

The Bible consistently outsells every book ever written. I could hardly wait to grab this book during the break at the conference.

I was sitting there, affected by the power of his words and thinking, *Man, I need to get this book!* I was thinking that if all 2,500 attending coaches and speakers want this book, we won't all get one. Those who wouldn't be able to buy one on the spot would have to order one and wait to receive their copy. I didn't think I could afford the patience to wait that long. I mean, not after all that Mr. Maxwell had just said.

I was sitting five tables or so away from the stage. I looked to the back of the room and saw that I would have to rush to where the books were being sold if I was going to be one of the lucky participants to buy the book that day. Before John Maxwell finished speaking, I was only half-listening, focusing instead on how I would get to the door. I eagerly made my way out of the room, and lo and behold; I saw a mass of people heading over to buy their books.

My calculations paid off: I had gotten there in time. I was lucky. Only a few individuals had made it there before me. They were ordering a variety of other titles. I wasn't interested in those. I wanted *The Greatest Story Ever Told*.

"Do you have *The Greatest Story Ever Told*?" I asked the attendant.

"Yes, we do," he answered.

"Can I have one, please?" I excitedly inquired.

"Sure!" said the attendant as he handed me a brand-new copy.

As I flipped the pages feverishly, I saw Mr. Maxwell's promised personal note in his handwriting. I also saw his signature. I grinned.

Then I flipped to the next page. The top of the page read, "Please, share your story with us." But that was not the page I was looking for. So I flipped a couple more pages as I struggled to get to find the correct page where the *real* content of the book started.

For a moment, I thought I had gone too far because I seemed to have fallen on some blank pages. I flipped backward. My findings were still the same—blank pages. I flipped some more, and it took me back to the page I had seen before. I again read the words in bold at the top of the page, which said, "Please, share your story with us."

Well, this does not make sense to me, I argued with myself, growing more anxious. I flipped forward again to see if I could find the table of contents, the foreword, the preface, the introduction, or chapter 1! *Something* that could help me know what the book was all about. It took a few more seconds for me to realize that the 248-page book was filled with blank pages!

I returned to Mr. Maxwell's note, reading it more slowly this time, not wanting to miss again what I had missed before.

"Dear Friend," began the note. "*The Greatest Story Ever Told* can only be written by you."

At the reading of this, my fingers froze as I pondered whether to buy the book. For just a moment, I was truly disappointed. This book was empty! There wasn't *any* story there, let alone *The Greatest Story Ever Told*. For some strange reason, I concluded, "Yes, I would buy this."

While still standing at the product table, I reread the words, "*The Greatest Story Ever Told* can only be written by you." At these words, the world *paused* for me. Though it took only a few seconds, it seemed like an eternity as I saw my whole life flash before me.

I saw my six-year-old self in my tiny village in the savannas of Cameroon, Central Africa, caring for my grandparents' herd of goats on the hillside. I thought about my village school that I walked about six miles to each day. I thought about the off-the-grid lifestyle we lived with no electricity or running water.

I saw my adult self, standing at the luggage carrousel of the Louis Armstrong International Airport in New Orleans, Louisiana, waiting for my bags. I had just arrived in the United States for the very first time. I had left my dear wife and our two children in my home country to pursue a graduate education.

I still could hear the sweet sounds of the jazz music that the airport sound system played gently in the background. I still could feel the beating of my heart within my chest. It beat out of fear and anxiety. You see, I had left my entire family behind in Africa to chase the dream of a U.S. graduate education. My wife was a stay-at-home mom; my kids were not yet of school age. I had left my family with no savings at all. In just a few days, I would need to pay thousands of dollars in graduate school tuition. Yet, all that I had to my name was $600! How was I going to make it in this country as a fresh new immigrant? Where would the tuition money come from? What about my wife and our two lovely children? How would they survive?

Many other thoughts came to my mind as I stood holding *The Greatest Story Ever Told*; too many thoughts to list here. Then I began to question, "What is there to tell about me?" "What would the world want to know about a shy, bullied, 'not enough' figure?"

"What is there to be admired?" "What is there to be said of him?"

Then I slowly began to think about the journey from *then* to *now*, and a gentle and warm excitement began to well up in me. It was at that moment that I decided to write my story: The greatest story that had yet to be told! The story of how I survived the darkness and conquered my fears. How I made it through many valleys and endured the depths. How I withstood my failures and weathered my deepest regrets. How I strove to make every one of my dreams come to pass. How I learned to make *today* count for me. And, finally, how these principles now help thousands that sit at our conferences and seminars or attend our mastermind and mentorship programs; how they make *today* count for them. In more than fifteen countries to date—from everyday people to leaders of nations and from students to corporate executives—it has been my privilege to teach these timeless principles.

This is the thought that birthed this book. It is a chronicle of simple principles I embraced that changed my life. I'm truly honored to share my story and those lessons with you.

INTRODUCTION

The Day Before Tomorrow represents one of the greatest lessons I have learned in all my life. It is an idea I have found to be simple yet profound. It is the notion that the greatest and most important day of your life is not tomorrow, nor is it yesterday. It is the idea that the greatest and most important day of your life is *today!*

When I decided in 2019 to schedule this book for the upcoming year, 2020, little did I know that the thought would turn out to be a heavenly conspiracy. For one thing, the principles discussed in this book would be tested in real-time by a global crisis—the coronavirus pandemic.

It barely took sixteen days from the time of the first suspected transmission of the COVID-19 virus in the United States in late February to the declaration of a national emergency in mid-March 2020. In another fifteen days, state after state would shut down due to "stay at home" orders. Life as we knew it in the United States—and the rest of the world—was over.

We found ourselves in a completely new world order that no one could have anticipated just days before. As the infection number rose from a few dozen to a million in just a few weeks and the death toll climbed to nearly a hundred thousand, it became relatively clear that our daily lives were never going to be the same again.

Community businesses we had grown to rely on shut down. Other services began to emerge. Those who had the resources and could sew began making face masks in their homes to sell or share. Some who had never sewn before taught themselves a new skill. Could anyone have ever imagined just yesterday that this would be in their future?

Global travel came to a screeching halt as travel restrictions were imposed. University teaching migrated online seemingly overnight. Grade-school children also transitioned to home-school learning. Parents who once relied on the school system as they commuted to work found their entire lives changed in an instant. They would learn how to become makeshift teachers to their children while figuring out how to keep them occupied during school hours. The COVID-19 pandemic proved that *anything* indeed is possible, and *anything* can change.

A thriving U.S. economy of early March 2020 plummeted to numbers comparable to the Great Depression in just three months. Twenty-six million people lost their employment within the same period. The future became uncertain. It became unpredictable.

At the time of the writing of this piece, no one knows what the next weeks and months may look like. Not even the health experts and scientists can tell for sure. Even though it's been said that we might have reached the peak of infection, no one can tell what exactly will happen.

People are getting tired of staying at home. Millions will have to face the new normal of no handshaking, public mask-wearing, and the six-foot physical distancing rule.

It's also unclear what the school system will look like when classes resume in the fall (if they resume at all!). Is homeschooling going to be the new norm? Are schools going to be safe enough for all? How will students maintain social distancing? When can we expect a cure? Is a vaccine in sight? These are but a few of the unknowns.

When it became apparent that no one could tell how long millions of people would remain confined to their homes, that millions would be infected, and that tens of thousands were going to die from the virus, we were all forced to learn how to live in the *moment*. We learned how to live a day at a time, *literally*. The *yesterday* we knew was gone, and even the tomorrow we anticipated was steeped in uncertainty. We could no longer rely on the escapism of yesterday or dwell in the fantasy of tomorrow. *Today* became all we had.

It was in the middle of this global crisis that the importance of focusing on the present moment became clear to all and sundry. Ruminating about the past or worrying about the future became a futile engagement. We had a global living example of the preciousness of *today*.

Many couldn't look back at the strong retirement savings of yesterday. They were gone! I heard a restaurant owner weep on the phone as she reflected on the income and investments that had just vanished. The joys of only a few weeks before were difficult to recall. *Yesterday* had become nearly useless. Some people who had thriving businesses before the crisis were now living in survival mode. Others who earned menial wages now benefitted temporarily from generous stimulus packages that provided more than they earned while working their jobs. Some still struggled to live in yesterday; others waited for tomorrow; however, many began to adjust and embrace the gift of *today*.

The hope of tomorrow seemed elusive. Preconceived notions of tomorrow flew out the window. There were no predefined rules to follow that could guarantee a bright future. People muddled through, attempting to find their way. Hours and hours of media coverage only shed more darkness on an already gloomy picture. Business deals would be canceled. Travel would be frozen. People were hoarding products and food in fear of what could happen next. No one seemed to be sure of what tomorrow had in store.

The only day they could count on was *today*!

I observed people from different nations, religions, creeds, and philosophies adjust to the crisis. I talked to people. I read stories of people from Asia, Europe, Africa, and the Americas as the crisis unfolded. It became apparent to me as the calamity went on that people's attitudes began to change. I noticed that people began to function better only when they had forgotten about yesterday, didn't focus much on tomorrow, and just embraced the day that was before them. Never did the "one day at a time" slogan ever ring more true!

Maybe this global crisis came to teach us a better way to think and live. Maybe it came to remind us that every day is a true gift that must be greeted with thankfulness and cheerfulness. Maybe it came to reconnect us with our humanity again. Maybe it came to show us that our most important moments are now, and our most important day is today.

This book is written for everyone who desires to tap into the power of the present moment. It is written for the one who wants to lay hold of the opportunities of today, rewrite yesterday, and create a new tomorrow.

The Day Before Tomorrow is written for anyone who has wrestled with—or continues to wrestle with—yesterday, has dreams for tomorrow, and is curious about exploring the gift of today. It is written for those who want today to deliver its promise of abundant and satisfying life, regardless of life's circumstances. This book is here for those who are ready and willing to embrace the greatest adventure of living a full and purposeful life.

CHAPTER 1

THE ILLUSION OF TOMORROW

"If the fight is tomorrow,
why then clench your fist today?"

Cameroonian proverb

Everyone thinks about tomorrow. Everyone believes in tomorrow. Yet no one has ever seen tomorrow, nor can anyone live tomorrow today. Tomorrow is not a given. And so goes a proverb from my homeland: "If the fight is tomorrow, why then clench your fist today?"

Living tomorrow today is like living with a clenched fist, preparing for a fight that will not happen until tomorrow. The truth is we don't know for sure that we will even be here tomorrow, let alone if there will be a fight tomorrow. When we spend our time worrying about and being anxious for tomorrow, we are missing the opportunities we have today, right here and right now. If we invest *all* of our actions in anticipation of what will happen tomorrow, the opportunities of today will pass right by us. They will slip away and be lost forever.

When our hands are clenched in fists, we push the people away who attempt to shake our hands in friendship and miss the opportunity to know what they could have brought into our lives. We can't be bothered because we are fully invested in preparing for the fight tomorrow. The person who is in front of us today is not important when we don't live for today. We cannot reach out to others in friendship, either. We are too focused on our fight tomorrow.

It's been said, "Yesterday is history, tomorrow is a mystery, today is a gift—that's the reason why it is called the present." But who among us has ever received a *present* with a clenched fist? Who of us has ever embraced a *gift* with closed hands? Can't we see that the gift of every minute, of every hour, of all the hours, of today meets the clenched-fisted individual unready and unprepared? How many more gifts can we afford to let fall by the wayside?

Imagine people watching us walking around with clenched fists. They may ask us, "Why are you walking that way with your fists clenched?" They cannot see the tomorrow we are preparing for. All they can see is a contorted body full of rage and anger. Imagine if you explained to them, "I have a great fight tomorrow." They will be surprised because they'll have no idea what you are talking about. They'll be embarrassed they attempted to reach out to you. The opportunity is lost to connect with others. We move on with our day, ignoring the potential of today, with our fists firmly clenched, waiting to be present in a predetermined conception of an uncertain tomorrow. We don't know that there will be a fight tomorrow, do we? There is no certain assurance that there will even be a tomorrow for us.

TOMORROW IS NOT GRANTED, SO DO NOT TAKE TODAY FOR GRANTED

My very good friend Kevin Taylor came to the consciousness of this reality about two and a half years ago. Kevin is not only my close friend but has also served as the lead pastor of our Silver Creek Church congregation for more than fourteen years. His wife Veronica, his adult children Benjamin and Becca, and his teenage son Isaac have grown to become family to me. I have even had the honor to speak alongside Kevin to hundreds of leaders in our leadership conferences in Africa.

On the evening of Thursday, January 25, 2018, I received a late-night phone call from Kevin's son Ben. The call was brief and straight to the point. Summarily, Ben told me, "My dad suffered a cardiac arrest during his Zumba class and has been rushed to the emergency room. Please, pray for him. And by the way, we haven't made this public just yet."

Kevin would later recall the events of that day.

The music in the gym was really loud as the Zumba class was starting to warm up. Compared to a normal class, the gym was packed. In addition to the regulars, there was the entire ladies' golf team and their coaches from the university where I teach. The team had just finished an abbreviated workout, and the coaches were looking for some additional aerobic training to provide the ladies.

3

Everyone began to mimic the movements of the teacher at the front of the class. The tempo of the music turned from warm-up to workout, and the intensity of the movements increased to reflect the rhythm of the Latin-flavored music.

Although unaware of it, only ninety seconds into the first song, as the class continued moving to the music, Kevin stood motionless and bent at the waist. He remembers wondering why the instructor appeared to be leaning in a strange direction.

His friend Molly and her husband Mike were on the other side of the class in the back row. Molly let out a scream as Kevin toppled forward face-first onto the rubbery material of the gym floor. Molly's scream signaled the instructor to stop the music.

Several of the students in the class came immediately to assess the situation. Looking past the blood flowing from the bridge of his nose where his glasses had cut deep into the skin, they were able to quickly determine that he had no pulse. One of the golfers mentioned that Kevin was already turning blue. Avery, a senior on the golf team that year, majoring in athletic training, took control of the situation, informing the others that she was starting cardiopulmonary resuscitation (CPR). She also directed the instructor to grab the gym's automated external defibrillator (AED) and one of her coaches to call 911.

Another class member, who worked on the cardiac floor of our local hospital, stepped into position opposite Avery to assist as well. Phil, the gym instructor, grabbed the AED from the wall. Phil remembered that, while giving a new employee a tour of the gym a few weeks earlier, he pointed out the AED unit as a formality and noted, "But we never use it." The exchange prompted him to wonder if it might be good to change out the battery on the unit, and so he did.

Avery's CPR training took over her thoughts and actions as she began counting out the first set of sixty chest compressions. After a quick rescue breath and a check for a pulse, Avery began another set of chest compressions. One more rescue breath and a pulse was detected, and he began breathing on his own. A couple of the young ladies from the golf team could be heard crying off to the side. Several minutes later, the first responder walked in the door carrying his AED.

Weeks later, the officer would tell Kevin's wife how glad he was that he didn't have to use his AED that evening and that everything was totally under control by the time he arrived just minutes after the call was made. Kevin's sense of humor wasn't damaged: Before the arrival of the ambulance, he was asking the instructor if he would get a refund because he wasn't able to finish the class!

Over the following twenty-four hours, numerous tests would be run, and it was determined that Kevin had suffered a cardiac arrest. It was described as the classic "widowmaker." While shoveling earlier that winter, Kevin had been running out of breath, but he didn't recognize this as a warning sign. It was determined that Kevin had two blockages that would require bypass surgery. Stents would not be effective due to the location of the blockages in the arteries.

It's hard to believe what happens during open-heart surgery. The patient's sternum is cut apart with a saw, and a jack is used to separate the ribs to create an opening for the surgeon to work.

In Kevin's case, the surgeons would need to harvest two veins from his body: One from the groin and the other from the inside of his chest wall. During surgery, his heart was placed on a heart pump, which would allow his doctors to complete the double bypass. Once the new veins were connected, his heart was taken off the pump. The doctors were pleased that the heart immediately functioned at one hundred percent capacity with the help of the newly replaced veins.

Over the following six months, Kevin would go through a long road to recovery. But he is one tough cookie. In September of the same year, only seven months after open-heart surgery, Kevin crossed the finish line of the Marquette Half Marathon (13.1 miles). One week later, Kevin and his son Ben would run a Tough Mudder event, completing a ten-mile distance run with twenty obstacles.

Kevin recounts that the cardiac arrest experience heightened his sense of how much his family needs him to live a godly example of a man who loves and serves his family with his whole heart.

"Although my wife would have taken care of my family and my adult children would certainly have survived; what about the teenage boy that would undoubtedly still need his father to teach him the many lessons of becoming a man?" he recalls questioning himself.

This purpose continues to drive him today. Kevin understands that there is no guarantee of tomorrow! He is more aware now of his mortality than ever before. Although heaven would be a serious promotion, he continues to work to stay healthy to live the best life possible today so that he can continue to influence his son, his family, his congregation, and his community.

Tomorrow is an illusion.

Never let the future disturb you. You will meet it, if you have to, with the same weapons of reason which today arm you against the present.

Marcus Aurelius

WE LEARNED IT THE HARD WAY

Kobe Bryant

We experienced this truth again with the tragic and unfortunate death of our beloved American basketball legend Kobe Bryant. Kobe was only forty-one years old when he and his thirteen-year-old daughter, Gianna, were killed in a helicopter crash while traveling to Gianna's basketball game, where Kobe was to coach. It's unlikely the nine passengers in the helicopter knew January 26, 2020, would be their last day.

Mrs. Vanessa Bryant lost her husband of nearly twenty years and her daughter on the same day—an unthinkable loss. It's highly unlikely she thought she would be raising their three surviving daughters—seventeen-year-old Natalia, three-year-old Bianka, and eight-month-old Capri—by herself. Tens of thousands of people flocked to the Staples Center, where Bryant starred for the Los Angeles Lakers during a twenty-year career that included five NBA championships, to pay their respects.

During the Grammy Awards in the Staples Center, on the day following his death, pop music legend Alicia Keys and the popular American R&B group Boyz II Men performed the song *It's So Hard to Say Goodbye to Yesterday* in tribute to Kobe Bryant.

All we can count on is today.

President John F. Kennedy

The world changed forever on November 22, 1963, when the thirty-fifth president of the United States, John F. Kennedy, was assassinated while riding in an open convertible in a presidential motorcade in Dallas, Texas. It has been said that the world lost its innocence that day. As a nation, we became deeply aware that tomorrow is not promised.

Jackie Kennedy likely thought she would be at her husband's side as he served the remainder of his historical presidency as the first Irish-Catholic and the youngest elected president ever. Mrs. Kennedy became a young widow with two small children. The nation that invested so much optimism in the future of President Kennedy's work for opportunity and advancement for all was now temporarily lost. The children who had no concept of death were now participating in their father's official presidential ceremonial funeral. Lyndon B. Johnson would become the thirty-sixth president of the United States. The tomorrow we believed in was lost as the nation embraced the reality of today.

Dr. Myles Munroe

Again, I learned this the hard way when one of my most admired leaders, Dr. Myles Munroe, passed. This spiritual giant, his wife, and eight others died in a plane crash on November 9, 2014, *en route* to a leadership conference. Dr.

Munroe was a Bahamian evangelist and ordained minister. He was an avid professor of the Kingdom of God, a highly-sought speaker, and a leadership consultant who founded and led the Bahamas Faith Ministries International (BFMI) and Myles Munroe International (MMI). He was also the author of numerous books. At fifty-nine years old, his plans spanned far into the future. I remember hearing Dr. Munroe say, "My next twenty years are all planned."

Dr. Munroe's adult children, Myles, Jr., and Charisa, lost their father, whom they had likely anticipated would be a doting grandfather to their children someday. Tens of thousands lost their spiritual leaders as Dr. Munroe and his wife, Ruth, co-pastors in Bahamas Faith Ministries International, perished.

The preceding are but a few examples that teach us that even the next minute is truly in the future.

Why do we struggle to accept that today is all we have? Why do we wrestle with the idea of making the most of today? Why can't we live fully, be present, and give all we have as we connect deeply with those around us?

It takes courage to face today. Not the same courage it takes to fight, but the courage to be vulnerable. The courage to be aware that we don't have it all figured out. Yes, true courage is to know that tomorrow is not promised—that the certainty of tomorrow is an illusion.

I realize that of the thousands and thousands of days that exist, there are only three days that truly exist—*yesterday, today,* and *tomorrow.* Every person alive has lived but one day already—*yesterday.* Every person alive is living but one day—*today.* If we are lucky, we may see a third day—*tomorrow.* In truth, none of us has the luxury to relive yesterday or to live in *tomorrow.* All we have is today! All we are guaranteed is *now.* This, to me, is a humbling thought—that the only day I have is *the day before tomorrow!*

Remember this truth: there is no one like you. You have unique gifts, skills, insights, tastes, preferences, intellect, physical abilities, and a sense of humor. There was no one like you before you were born. There will never be anyone like you again. Today will bring experiences, people, and things that will vanish tomorrow and become your yesterday. If you must live in *tomorrow,* let it be the tomorrow you talked about yesterday. Forget about tomorrow; it does not exist—just yet. Live today. Ask yourself this question: "What shall I do with this gift of today?"

TAKE YOUR TURN:
HOW CAN YOU MAKE TODAY COUNT?

1. List five ways in which you take *tomorrow* for granted.

_____

_____

_____

_____

_____

_____

2. If you knew for sure that *tomorrow* is not a given, list five things you would do differently.

_____

_____

_____

_____

_____

_____

3. What can you do today, so you do not take *today* for granted?

• In your personal life

_____

_____

_____

- In your family/relational life

_____

_____

_____

- In your career life

_____

_____

_____

- In your business/professional life

_____

_____

_____

4. What action(s) can you take daily to avoid living in the *illusion of tomorrow?*

_____

_____

_____

_____

_____

_____

_____

CHAPTER 2

THE DELUSION OF YESTERDAY

*"There is nothing about your past
that determines your future."*

John C. Maxwell

Every living person has a yesterday: a memory that evokes either a sense of joy or a sense of horror, depending on what their yesterday was all about. In my travels, readings, and interactions with people, I have found that the past can be a force of good or evil. Some people use their past against themselves. Others use their past as building blocks for creating good in their own lives and the world. What is true about everyone is that we all have good pasts and bad pasts.

It is my observation that every successful person has had a failure in the past; they simply choose to walk past that past. I have also noticed that all those who experienced "failures" have had the opportunity to succeed; unfortunately, they turned down the option. So whether we are successful or unsuccessful, we all are products of our past. Each of us can choose to leverage our past to work for us or against us.

A few weeks ago, I listened to the story of two

brothers. Let's call them Greg and Jeff. They were raised by a father who could best be described as irresponsible. Unfortunately, their father had many issues. He was not present in their lives and was not a reliable partner to their mother. He also endured a fierce struggle with addiction. According to their story, their father was heartless, unkind, and abusive to Greg and Jeff. Over the years, the two brothers grew to become adults and lead lives of their own, despite the shadow of their past.

What intrigued me about their story was the diametrically different outcomes of the brothers' lives. Greg became a very successful family man and a physician. He was financially stable, a productive member of his community, and well-loved by many who knew him. All who knew him thought he was the personification of all that a successful individual should be. His medical practice saved the lives of many in the community. In addition to all his success, he somehow found the time to start a grassroots organization to take care of homeless and abused children. Greg was one of those people you would easily nominate as a *CNN Hero* (a news segment that recognizes those who influence positive change in the world).

Jeff, on the other hand, became the kind of individual you might see on the evening news police report. He made all the wrong choices, was perpetually under the influence of illegal substances, had a couple of run-ins with the law, spent time in and out of jail, and developed a long-term debilitating health condition.

When the two brothers were each asked what in the development of their lives had influenced them the most, they both pointed to the same thing—their irresponsible father.

When Greg told the story of being raised by his father, he shared examples of the man he did not want to be. He remembers his mother crying often and that he and his brother rarely had enough to fulfill their basic needs. He recalls days at school when his father would forget to pick him up because he was under the influence of drugs or alcohol. He remembers not wanting to bring his friends home. He recalls his father mocking and beating him. Greg shared, "If you had the kind of father that I had, you would have no option but to become the person I am today." Greg went on to discuss how, after periods of reflection, he grew to have empathy for his father. He learned his father had issues in his past he unfortunately never healed from. Greg admitted, "I don't admire my father, but I have found a way to love him for who he is." Greg talked about his past without much emotion. When he told the story, it was a very distant memory.

Interestingly, Jeff, his brother, said almost the same thing. He reflected, "Man, if you knew my dad, you wouldn't question why I turned out this way." Jeff had similar memories to Greg; however, the wounds were very fresh. He talked about the indignities that he suffered from his father in the present tense. The pain of being left at school or finding his father passed out on the couch was as real for him today as they were when he was just a ten-year-old boy. He recalled the hunger and the humiliation. It was obvious that Jeff did not want to be like his father either. He shared he wouldn't be "weak" like his father and that he could "handle" partying once in a while. When Jeff spoke, his face was contorted in pain, and his body was tense as if he were ready to jump into a fight at any time.

An identical past led to different outcomes. Why is that the case? The reasons are more clear than might be suspected. Each individual has the power to decide to leverage their past to make positive progress. They also have the power to let the shadow of their past stall them, forever limiting their opportunities. Both Greg and Jeff had experiences in their life that they received differently. Jeff was too angry to recognize that there was help around him if he wanted it. He discussed feeling better when he had time to "dry out" in prison. He lamented that he had a nice girlfriend who left him and a child he didn't know.

Greg also shared that he experimented with drugs and alcohol in school. He discussed that, in his younger years, he desperately wanted to be part of the fun. He recognized that when he took substances, he felt like a different person and even acted in ways that surprised him. He stated that feeling the effects of the drugs on his body inspired him to want to go to medical school to learn more about how drugs positively affect people.

We have the power of choice to determine whether our past affects us positively or negatively. Why would we ever choose the negative?

YESTERDAY IS GONE, WE CANNOT RELIVE IT

I am greatly inspired by the words in Og Mandino's book *The Greatest Salesman in the World*. This excerpt beautifully illustrates that yesterday is true, gone.

> *Can sand flow upward in the hourglass? Will the sun rise where it sets and set where it rises? Can I relive the errors of yesterday and right them? Can I call back yesterday's wounds and make them whole? Can I become younger than yesterday? Can I take back the evil that was spoken, the blows that were struck, the pain that was caused? No. Yesterday is buried forever, and I will think of it no more.*

> Og Mandino
> *The Greatest Salesman in the World*

Take a minute to let this truth sink in.

How much of today are you letting yesterday eat up? What is your plan to keep yesterday where it belongs—in the past?

You may protest, "What if yesterday was great and its memories still inspire me?" If that is true for you, wonderful; you are very lucky. However, realize that even a positive past has vanished. Those that linger in the warmth of a glowing past risk missing the opportunity of the present. They may be holding on so tightly to the memories of what once was that they are now missing what is. Do not let your focus on and occupation with the past rob you of the possibilities of today. The memories you create today will soon be your yesterday.

I have had my struggles with yesterday. I was the first of six children born to my single-parent mom. I questioned why we suffered hardship, why we had no food, why we lacked the money to take care of my tuition, or why we were barely surviving. I'd wonder why my father wasn't present in my life. I'd compare myself to some of my friends who had loving relationships with their fathers and seemed to have enough resources to live an easy and stress-free life. I was sad because I couldn't dress as elegantly as the other children at school.

I would spend time considering my past, thinking that life would have been very different for me if I had more advantages. I'd convince myself that my life would have been entirely different if I had a different past. I vividly remember classmates from elementary school who came from extremely well-to-do families. They came to school driven in the family car while I walked six miles each day. The other children had ready access to textbooks and had snacks during break time. Remember, I grew up in Africa, where every child is not granted every resource.

As a child, I envied these classmates. I would feel sorry for myself and ask, "Why am I so unlucky?" It's shocking for me to note that the advantages those classmates had during childhood had no bearing on where some of them ended up today. Some didn't take advantage of their head start in life. It would appear they imagined their privileged upbringing would inevitably secure them a brighter future.

It did not.

When I became a teenager, I had an appetite for excessive drinking and some smoking. Unfortunately, I had witnessed several family members suffer from addiction. I somehow found the strength at just nineteen years old to choose to stop using substances—I call it my *divine turnaround.*

The shadow of my underprivileged past lingered with me as I grew into adulthood. When I was in my thirties, I still found myself relapsing into bouts of anger and regret over my past. I was angry at a father who was absent from my life. I regretted that my mom struggled with addictions and challenges of her own and could not be the loving and available mother I longed for. The feelings that developed in my teen years of not "being enough"—and feelings of rejection and pain—continually crossed my mind. Think about this: By the time I was thirteen, I had lived in three different households in four different towns—I was constantly in a new home atmosphere and culture. This constant change caused me to live in a perpetual state of learning my environment. What worked for one household did not necessarily work for another. It was hard to develop a productive routine that helped me make progress.

This past made me waste the opportunities that were right before me by living in the pain of my yesterday. Meanwhile, those experiences happened many years ago and, in reality, had no reflection on the man I was in the present. For some reason, at that time, I was choosing not to let those limiting beliefs go.

The day I realized that I could not change my yesterday was very liberating, but it did not happen suddenly. It did not happen until I learned that my today could be different from my yesterday—if I wanted it to be. The illumination of this realization hit me when I was nineteen years old and decided to start a brand-new life, far away from my controlling addictions. This was my *divine turnaround,* as I mentioned before. It's now been nearly thirty years since I made that decision, and it feels like I've never known alcohol or cigarettes in my life. As I started to accept new thoughts and relinquish limiting beliefs, I discovered that successful people keep past failures perpetually in the past. This empowering thought began to gradually free me and allow me to successfully turn the lessons of the memories of my past into empowering thoughts that now help me to live a full life.

Whenever we limit the past to the past, it allows us room to take on *today*'s tasks. The ability to put the past in perspective is, therefore, critical for leading a successful life today.

FIVE MYTHS ABOUT YESTERDAY

We tend to believe the stories we continually tell ourselves. That is one reason our widely-held but false beliefs and ideas can adversely affect us. I have found the following myths to be deleterious to those who possess them.

1. **I Am a Victim of Yesterday.**
   It's easy to play the victim. It affords us an easy escape from reality. It numbs us to the things we need addressed in our own lives and affords us lethargy.

2. **A Successful Yesterday Guarantees Tomorrow.**
   No matter how wonderful yesterday was, it is gone! It is impossible to benefit today from events and experiences that do not exist today.

3. **An Unsuccessful Yesterday Seals Tomorrow's Fate.**
   Yesterday's failures do not have to cross over into tomorrow. People not only make decisions, but decisions also make people. The first decision to make when you wake up to a new day is to decide that it will be the end of yesterday. Yesterday's experience mustn't be your reality today or tomorrow.

4. **Yesterday Does Not Matter.**
   Yesterday cannot be ignored. It carries in it the baseline for your wisdom if leveraged correctly. Think of it this way: Your yesterday gave birth to your today. Are you satisfied with today? Are you happy with the results yesterday has inflicted on today? If you aren't, you can change the inputs of today. One of these inputs is how you think of yesterday. If you are happy with yesterday, you can replicate its fruits today. But in all you do, be careful not to discount yesterday's potential to affect today, for better or for worse.

5. **Yesterday Is Everything.**
   Yesterday is *not* everything! It's just a segment of the story. There's still today. No matter how good yesterday was, it is still not enough. No matter how terrible it was, the other part of the story has yet to be told. The profound truth is that you can use today to cancel out yesterday. Yesterday is not all that there is.

FIVE TRUTHS ABOUT YESTERDAY

Falsities can only be conquered by enduring truths. We only defeat a lie by a truth. Therefore, every story of yesterday that is told must be filtered through the lens of verity. I have found that there are five essential truths about yesterday.

1. **Yesterday Is Gone.**
   This point may seem trivial mentally, but in real life, it usually isn't. I know many who still hold onto

yesterday for some reason. Sometimes it's the joys that yesterday brought to them. Do you know how they talk about the "good old days"? At other times, it is the sadness and trauma yesterday inflicted. People may have lived through abuse, neglect, bullying, or some other debilitating drawback. I mean, life happens! Nevertheless, without making light of anyone's past, whether good or bad, it is still the past. The past is past! Let's leave it where it belongs—the past. Today is a new day. Embrace and live it.

2. **Nothing Can Be Done to Change Yesterday.**
   It is impossible to change yesterday. I mean, can the leopard change his spots? Once you embrace this realization, the feeling is quite liberating. So make peace with your past. What is probably more empowering is recognizing that today can be entirely different from yesterday. But that's a choice we have to make. Nonetheless, once we fully accept that our past cannot be changed, we can begin to live right today.

3. **You Can Benefit from Yesterday.**
   Anyone can take advantage of yesterday and use it to become better. Yesterday's dealings provide a baseline of wisdom for today. The wisdom of yesterday is a gift readily available to us today. How we use it is up to us. The story of the two brothers, Greg and Jeff, demonstrates that lesson for us.

4. **Yesterday Can Stall or Propel Positive Progress Today.**
   The impact of yesterday on today cannot be overemphasized. Yesterday can be a force for good or

evil, depending on how we leverage it. The important choice we make will shape the today we live in.

5. **Yesterday + Reflection = Good Insight.**
Yesterday carries valuable lessons that can transform a life, regardless of whether they were painful or pleasant. Yesterday's experiences must therefore be evaluated through reflection to gain new and better perspectives. Imagine Jeff in our story above. What if he realized that he could help others struggling with addiction, having difficult relationships, and doing time in jail—just as he had? Who better than Jeff to help someone navigate that difficult terrain?

The way to tap into yesterday's wisdom is to reflect on yesterday's experiences while we ask pertinent questions. The result is powerful insights that push us forward and allow each of us to live as full a life as possible, the life we were meant to live.

Permit me to ask, "Are you using your *past*, or is your *past* using you?"

TAKE YOUR TURN:
HOW CAN YOU MAKE TODAY COUNT?

1.   List any *myth(s) about yesterday* that tend to affect you the most.

_____

_____

_____

_____

_____

_____

_____

2.   List any truth(s) about *yesterday* that you can easily take advantage of to help you live a better life.

_____

_____

_____

_____

_____

_____

_____

3.   What can you do today so that you do not live in *yesterday?*

· In your personal life

_____

_____

_____

· In your family/relational life

_____

_____

_____

· In your career life

_____

_____

_____

· In your business/professional life

_____

_____

_____

4. What action(s) can you take daily to overcome
the *delusion of yesterday?*

_____

_____

_____

_____

_____

_____

_____

CHAPTER 3

THE CRITICAL INTERSECTION: TODAY

*"Today is the tomorrow that we talked about yesterday,
and the yesterday that we will recall tomorrow."*

Madison Ngafeeson

In the December 1960 NFL Championship Game, the Green Bay Packers gave up their lead late in the fourth quarter of the game against the Philadelphia Eagles. There was no logical reason for the team to lose this game. They had led consistently for three quarters. It's likely the fans and the sports announcers were ready to proclaim the Green Bay Packers the 1960 NFL Champions. The game was highly anticipated, as both the Philadelphia Eagles and the Green Bay Packers were underdogs and had been struggling for two years in their respective East and West Conferences. But here they were, facing each other in a battle for the coveted national championship.

Over sixty-seven thousand fans filled the stadium, including seven thousand temporary seats, which were added to accommodate the demand to experience the game in person.[1] The Eagles came into the game with a 10–2

---

1 Longman, Jere *Eagles 1960 Victory was an NFL Turning Point, New York Times,* January 6, 2011

record. The Green Bay Packers started the season strong but slumped midseason and ended up with an 8−4 record. Vince Lombardi, a relatively unknown coach at the time, joined the Packers after being an assistant coach with the New York Giants and turned the team around in the final weeks of the season, earning the Packers their spot in the 1960 NFL Championship. It was 48 degrees Fahrenheit on December 26, 1960, at Franklin Field in Philadelphia, Pennsylvania, creating difficult circumstances for both teams. The ground was frozen in spots but melting in others, leaving puddles for the players to navigate during play.[2] The Eagles had not won a championship game since 1949, and the Packers had not won since 1944. The game was set to start at noon. There was great concern that the contentious game would go into overtime, forcing the players to play in the dark and perhaps necessitating sudden-death overtime where whichever team scored first would win.

As sportswriter Joseph Sheehan aptly summarized in his *New York Times* article published early the next morning, the Eagles surprisingly defeated the Packers 17−13, although the Packers were favored to win. Eagle Ted Dean slammed across the end zone for the deciding points from five yards out on a sweep around Green Bay's right end, behind a crushing block by fellow Eagle Gerry Huth. Dean

---

2 Sheehan, Joseph, Eagles Win, 17-13, to take Pro Title; 58-Yard Return Kick-Off Helps Defeat Packers 5 Yard End Sweeps Decides 17-3 67,325 See Dean's 58-Yard Return of Kick-Off Start Eagles' Winning Drive, *New York Times* December 27, 1960

set the winning drive in motion by sprinting fifty-eight yards to Green Bay's thirty-nine-yard line with a kickoff.

With their powerful running game, which accounted for 223 yards, the Packers controlled the ball for long intervals. However, the Packers lacked the decisiveness to act when presented with the opportunity to win. The Eagles, who only ran forty-eight scrimmage plays compared to the Packers' seventy-seven, did a better job of cashing in on their chances.

It was a sore loss for the Packers!

It marked the lone playoff defeat for Coach Vince Lombardi before his Packers team went on to establish a dynasty. How did Coach Lombardi create such an astounding success after suffering such a devastating loss? A legendary success we still reference today?

In the following year, in July of 1961, Coach Lombardi knew that yesterday was gone. On the first day of training camp, Lombardi stood before his team. He looked into the eyes of men who had come so close to winning it all in the previous season, and what he had to say was as shocking as the loss itself.

Coach Lombardi's words on the opening day of training would stupefy his team and literally change the face of football. Holding a football in his hand, he said to the team, "Gentlemen...this is a football." Wow! Talk about going back to basics!

These words were likely not easy for the team to hear. Lombardi's squad had been ruminating about that loss for the past six months. They were probably feeling pretty badly about themselves. They had endured teasing and some tough press during the post-game analysis. They had faced their wives, their children, their family, their friends, and the fans. They, without a doubt, had gone through their share of the cycle of grief—from anger, sadness, disappointment, and self-blame, to ultimately, hopefully, acceptance.

Now Coach Lombardi stood before the team, explaining the very basics of the game. He put their yesterday firmly behind them and was teaching them the lesson about embracing the day they had before them. The team now needed to get excited to get back to work and take the next step in their development as a team to prepare to win the next championship. They were humbled.

In his best-selling book, *When Pride Still Mattered*, author David Maraniss explains what happened when Lombardi walked into training camp in the summer of 1961.

> *He (Coach Lombardi) took nothing for granted. He began a tradition of starting from scratch, assuming that the players were blank slates who carried over no knowledge from the year before...*
>
> David Maraniss, *When Pride Still Mattered*

Lombardi even taught the players how to put on their socks and tie their shoes! Six months later, the Packers beat the New York Giants 37–0 to win the 1961 NFL Championship. On top of that, over seven years, Lombardi led the Packers to three World Championships and two Super Bowls.

So what's the lesson? Yesterday's failure does not matter if you are willing to pay the price of success today. Every day can be a new day if you choose to go back to the basics of what it takes to reconstruct your life all over again. Tomorrow only belongs to those who have learned to sweep clean the ruins of yesterday and to leave them in the past. Tomorrow belongs to those who will embrace and rebuild today.

Today is the critical intersection.

THE ART OF A NEW START

As Coach Lombardi taught his players, I feel that every human being needs to learn the *art of a new start*. The art of a new start is to begin each day with the 'football of life' in my hands and to say to myself, "Madison, this is *today*!"

Now, replace my name with your name and say out loud, "(*Your name*), this is *today*!"

Repeat this statement a couple of times until it means

something to you—"(*Your name*), this is *today!*" When I did this exercise the first time, I felt a couple of things happen inside me. When I started saying this, five key perspectives began to emerge in my life. When I say, "Madison, this is today!" I am:

- Reminding myself that today is *not* a continuation of yesterday.

- Affirming that the day I have before me is entirely new—the likes of which I have never seen.

- Committing to approaching today as being entirely different from yesterday and unlike any day I may ever see again.

- Giving yesterday a firm boundary line and demarcating what thoughts, feelings, and actions belong in today.

- Recognizing that today is the intersection of yesterday and tomorrow.

Living today is like living in the crosshairs because *what was* and *what will be* find their intersection in *what is.*

I learned this lesson firsthand as a new immigrant in the United States of America. As I noted briefly in the preface, I found myself standing at the luggage carousel at the Louis Armstrong New Orleans International Airport in Louisiana, waiting to collect my bags.

Sweet, gentle jazz music was playing in the background. Although the music was soothing, my heart was pounding in my chest. I had left my dear wife and our two precious children in my homeland of Cameroon to pursue graduate education in the U.S. I had been hopeful that I would be able to secure an academic scholarship when I started my application for graduate school. However, just a few months before, I would go for a visa interview at the U.S. Embassy in Yaounde, Cameroon. I learned that an academic scholarship would no longer be possible.

I was left with the critical decision of either postponing my admission date until the following year or taking the risk of shouldering the responsibility of the huge expense involved in paying for tuition and my living expenses abroad.

"What do you think we should do?" I remember asking my wife.
"Are there any other hopeful options?" she replied.
"As far as I know, the only other option is to defer admission for another year," I replied.
"No, we cannot do that. This is an opportunity of a lifetime. Let's figure out how to make this work," she said.

Knowing that my wife had my back was critical in my decision to move forward, regardless of what lay ahead. Even though I had her support and steadfast faith in me, standing at the airport in New Orleans with only $600 to my name while facing a huge tuition bill in the thousands of dollars, which was due in the following week or so, was downright frightening.

Living today, fully knowing that yesterday is gone and we do not know what awaits us in the future, is simultaneously both a simple and complex thought. I have found the following best practices to help keep me focused on remembering today is all we have.

HOW TO LIVE AND LEAD TODAY

1. **Understand that today is the end of yesterday and the start of tomorrow.** Today is the harvest of the seeds we planted yesterday and the seed of what is to come tomorrow. Today is the focal point of life.

When Coach Lombardi accepted the opportunity to coach The Green Bay Packers, he was a relatively unknown assistant coach. He did not let his history stop him from creating the legacy of the Green Bay Packers' championship in 1961. He also was not deterred by the devastating and unexpected loss during the NFL 1960 Championship. He put the past in the past; grabbing the opportunity of going back to basics, he built a formidable and winning team. Unfortunately, Coach Lombardi died from an aggressive form of cancer on September 3, 1970. It is said that his only regret on his deathbed was that he wished he could've done more. He died still wanting to engage his *today*!

2. **Take every intersection in life as an important decision moment.** When you find yourself at life's intersection, it is time to make a decision.

Conquistador Hernán Cortéz demonstrates the importance of making life-altering decisions when they truly matter. He was sent by Diego Velázquez de Cuéllar, the governor of Cuba, to dominate the fierce Aztec empire, which ruled Central and Northern Mexico from ad 1345 to ad 1521 Cortéz followed several previously unsuccessful attempts to overtake the Aztec empire. The Aztecs were known as skilled warriors and, until this time, had remained undefeated. Cortéz, leading his somewhat skeptical legion of five hundred soldiers, knew the only way to be successful was to eliminate the possibility of failure.

He famously ordered his soldiers to "scuttle their ships," and legend further tells that the ships were also burned for good measure, assuring there was no way the soldiers could retreat. His men, filled with concern, asked, "How will we return home?" Conquistador Cortéz replied with full confidence, "You will sail the Aztecs' ships home." The only option for his soldiers was either to win or die at the hands of the Aztecs. And win, they did.

Unless we "burn the ships" of yesterday through critical decision-making, we will never become serious about taking today head-on.

3. **Use today to cancel the yesterday you do not like.** Today can cancel yesterday, no matter what yesterday was.

The night of August 27, 1963, proved to be a sleepless one for Reverend Martin Luther King, Jr. He was due to give a speech at the Lincoln Memorial on August 28, so he stayed up late preparing notes for the big moment. As he was delivering his speech the following day, a gospel singer by the name of Mahalia Jackson, who was standing near his side, shouted, "Tell them about the dream, Martin!" King paused and went off-script. His decision in that moment changed the course of history. He delivered the famous I have a Dream speech, which is still regarded as one of the greatest speeches of all time.

I often wonder what would have happened if King had adhered to his script from the night before. What if King had not seized the moment? History as we know it would be different. That, to me, epitomizes the power of taking advantage of the moment to rewrite history forever.

4. **Use today to extend the yesterday you want to see.** If yesterday was really good and wonderful, plan to build upon it.

Although Kobe Bryant was one of the most successful National Basketball Association players of all time, he never relied on his successful past to shape his future. He knew that each day was a blank page to be written upon. He was always shrewdly aware that his competitors might have the same discipline. Kobe described waking up to practice every day at 4:00 a.m. He explained that no one was up at that time, and it added two more hours of practice to his day. Kobe had kept this discipline from his high school days. The only person who would be available to practice with him was the high school basketball coach. Kobe benefited from additional one-on-one guidance from his coach in the early hours of the morning that no other players had. He shared that if his coach wasn't available, he would coax the school's janitor to come and play with him. He also used his lunch hour to play while the other teenagers were enjoying lunch and recess. He described his discipline as the "mamba mentality." He recalled that if he wasn't using his talents to their greatest extent every day, he felt guilty for wasting the opportunity.[3]

A successful yesterday can serve as a foundation for continued success if correctly leveraged with the principle of consistency.

5. **Use today to sow new seeds for tomorrow.** Every day of our lives begins with a huge bag of seeds in our hands. We can choose to sow them or not. However, one thing is clear. Every action we take today will shape our tomorrow in significant ways.

At the time of the writing of this book, the COVID-19 pandemic has been and continues to be a real challenge.

---

3 TedX Shanghai Salon. *The Power of the Mind.* July 25, 2016

It radically changed people's schedules and altered routines in ways we could never have imagined. Before the pandemic, I never would have believed it would be possible that I would be unable to access my office for more than ninety days in a row!

I was suddenly forced to work from home. My life and everything I was used to changed overnight. I had to learn how to efficiently work from home, embrace new technology, and navigate the new demands of telework. I had to adjust and make the best use of my newly found time. The hours I used to spend commuting, traveling to meetings, and going to events were now free to use. I now had the responsibility of helping three children manage their twenty-four-hour schedule—learning online, missing their sports activities, and contact with friends— all while trying to figure out my schedule.

I knew I couldn't lose sight of the goals I had for the future. I knew that one day, the current situation would be past, and all I would have in my hands was the harvest of whatever I sowed today. Hence, I began to be intentional about time spent with my family, moments invested in self-development, and hours dedicated to serving others in my community and around the world. I had to adjust to a "new" day and see the circumstances before me through a fresh perspective.

I expect that the seeds sown in these challenging times

will yield a pleasant harvest for the future. We all must become intentional about the inputs of today, as they will inescapably generate the outputs of tomorrow.

6. **Maximize today by asking yourself the right questions.**

   o **What can I do to add value to myself?** Ultimately, an individual can only give what they have. To add value to others, we must first add value to ourselves. Doesn't the Golden Rule dictate that we do to others what we would have them do to us? This rule presupposes that we understand and possess self-love, something that is easy to overlook. The wisdom of the Golden Rule demonstrates that if we do not love ourselves, it is impossible for us to love and serve others. Therefore, take the important step of adding value to yourself every day.

   o **What can I do to add value to my significant relationships?**
   Just as it is easy for us to take for granted the love we need to give to ourselves, we sometimes overlook the importance of consciously adding value to our most significant relationships. It would have been easy to become frustrated spending 24/7 with my three children during the pandemic lockdown, and I must admit, there were moments of frustration for all. But once we all adjusted to the schedule and the new normal, many blessings began to emerge. They learned more about me and my

work. They saw me as a professional and not just as their dad. I was able to learn more about their daily struggles, their hopes, and their interactions. My wife, children, and I all learned how to navigate our space, keeping our connections strong, and allow each other room to grow and develop individually. Had the pandemic never happened, we might never have had the opportunity to connect in these meaningful new ways.

We can use today to add value to the relationships that mean the most to us.

○ **What can I do to add value to the people I serve?** The richness of life unfolds when we live our best selves in the service of others. It was a sweet delight when, amid the COVID-19 pandemic, we were able to join a team of others and serve three hundred families in our community with fresh food through Feeding America. It allowed us to turn our focus from the devastation of the pandemic to the beauty of the shared humanity that we were missing because of the shutdown.

Every day is an opportunity to plant the seeds of possibilities in others. When we capture all of the possibilities of today, it is impossible to take the fruitfulness of our daily interactions for granted. As we grasp the power of each day, we can maximize our gifts for the greatest good of others. One other thing that I was able to do during the pandemic that brought me joy was to speak to different groups of people from around the world and assist them in dealing with the pandemic. I delivered several teachings on "How to survive and thrive in challenging times." I was amazed how audiences in Africa, Europe, and America received this message. It was a true joy. The message helped them deal with fear, engage in studying the situation, and invest in developing efficiencies and productivity with their time.

○ **What can I do to add value to my community and world?**
It was John F. Kennedy who said, "Ask not what your country can do for you; ask what you can do for your country." When we make a conscious decision to add value to the community and society in which we live, life takes on a brand-new meaning. It is evident that when we live a life far beyond our selfish desires and seek the good of others, life opens to us in unprecedented ways. To maximize the day, we must seek opportunities to add value to the greater world beyond us.

Albert Einstein summed up the concept of living in today with these beautiful words:

"Learn from yesterday, live for today, hope for tomorrow."

TAKE YOUR TURN:
HOW CAN YOU MAKE TODAY COUNT?

1.   List any *myth(s) about yesterday* that tend to affect you
the most.

_____

_____

_____

_____

_____

_____

_____

2.   List any *truth(s) about yesterday* that you can easily take
advantage of to help you live a better life.

_____

_____

_____

_____

_____

_____

3.   What can you do today to ensure you do not waste today
living in *yesterday*?

• In your personal life

_____

_____

_____

• In your family/relational life

_____

_____

_____

• In your career life

_____

_____

_____

• In your business/professional life

_____

_____

_____

4. What action(s) can you take daily to overcome the *delusion of yesterday?*

_____

_____

_____

_____

_____

_____

CHAPTER 4

LOOK FORWARD FOR INSPIRATION

"Any fool can count the seeds in an apple. Only God can count all the apples in one seed."

Robert H. Schuller (1926-2015),
American Christian televangelist, pastor,
motivational speaker, and author

Approximately 2100 BC, an ancient patriarch of the Jewish people by the name of Abram (also known as Abraham) was visited by the God of the Jews, according to the Holy Bible.[4] Abram was seventy-five years old, and his wife was sixty-five when he saw the vision. The story goes on to tell that the God of the Jews promised Abram and his wife that they would have a child. This shocked the couple as they were both ways beyond the physical age of childbearing. Unfortunately, not only was Abram's wife, Sarai (also known as Sarah), significantly passed childbearing age, but she was also barren. The prospect of them having children appeared to be impossible.

One day God appeared to Abram in a vision and said, "Do not be afraid, Abram. I am your shield, your very great reward." To which Abram replied, "What can you give me since I remain childless and the one who will inherit

---

4 Genesis 15, New International Version

my estate is Eliezer of Damascus? You have given me no children, so a servant in my household will be my heir." God retorted, "This man will not be your heir, but a son who is your own flesh and blood. Your son will be your heir."

In the vision, God took Abram outside and said, "Look up at the sky and count the stars—if indeed you can count them." Then he said to him, "So shall your offspring be."

History notes that when Abram saw his future in the stars and all the potential he was promised, he deeply believed in God. He truly believed without a doubt that he could conceive a child with his over-aged, barren wife. He held strongly to the belief that they would become the patriarchs of an innumerable race of people. When Abram was a hundred years old and his wife was ninety, they had their son, Isaac, who became the patriarch of the Jewish nation.

The stars in the Abram story represent all the possibilities of the future. When Abram saw the countless stars and began to accept God's promise, the impossibility of age, barrenness, and a biological clock did not seem to matter much. The mental picture of the myriad of stars spoke of the possibility of tomorrow's opportunities. Nevertheless, he would have to believe in this future enough to act on its potential today.

Miracles happen when we have the faith to allow the picture of the future to inspire us to act on the possibility of today's impossibilities.

THE POWER OF HOPE

I had my own experience with being exposed to the possibilities of hope on May 5, 2007. I was part of a small group of student leaders selected by my university to attend the National Conference of Black Mayors in Baton Rouge, Louisiana. The then-presidential candidate, Mr. Barack Obama, was the special guest speaker. Though candidate Obama was quite a rising star within the Democratic Party, I knew nothing about him. I wasn't expecting anything more than a huge gathering of leaders from around the United States of America.

I had no idea at the time that this trip would turn out to be a very symbolic experience for me. As a new immigrant student from Africa, I was just glad to be in the company of great minds. I was very pleased just to be in such an uplifting and inspiring atmosphere. I was just taking in all the sights and sounds of my surroundings and enjoying the pleasant experience of traveling with my peer leaders.

The energy shifted as Mr. Obama was introduced. Music blasted throughout the large room; spotlights shone brightly on the podium. The curtains rustled behind the main stage. I felt I couldn't risk blinking, lest I miss out on the slightest bit of the exuberant action in the room. The air was thick with eager anticipation. As Candidate Obama emerged from behind the curtains, the room erupted with roaring applause, joyful shouts, and a standing ovation accompanied by loud background music. Obama waved at the crowd as he nodded, "Thank you." I could tell something great was about to happen.

As the crowd quieted, he started his speech. "It is an honor to be here at Southern University," he remarked. He then congratulated the mayors for the work they do in the cities of America—both great and small. He applauded their hard work, especially in times of disaster—like Hurricane Katrina, which had devastated the city of New Orleans and killed nearly 2,000 people just two years before.

He then began to tell the story of a pregnant woman from the extremely dangerous city of Compton, California, who was shot in the abdomen. The bullet penetrated her skin and womb and became lodged in her unborn child's upper limb. He shared details of the battle in the hospital to save the life of the mother and the unborn child with the bullet in its arm. The baby had to be delivered prematurely to save its life. The child survived. He concluded his story by remarking that, even though the bullet would be removed and the arm stitched, the child would still have to live with a bullet-scarred arm forever.

He then added that this story was not so unusual. He pointed out how "quiet riots" were taking place in similar cities all over the United States, where hope had dissipated, and a sense of disconnect had set in. He noted, "If you had gone to any street corner in Chicago or Baton Rouge or

Selma or Trenton or Arcola, Mississippi, you would have found the same young men and women without hope, without prospects, and without a sense of destiny other than life on the edge—the edge of the law, the edge of the economy, the edge of family structures and communities."

Obama continued, "Despair takes hold and young people all across this country look at the way the world is and believe that things are never going to get any better." He shared that they begin to tell themselves, "My school will always crumble. There will never be a good job waiting for me to excel at. There will never be a place I can be proud of, and I can afford to call my home." He relayed that "Despair quietly simmers and makes it impossible to build strong communities and neighborhoods. And then one afternoon a jury says, 'not guilty' (to a police officer charged with a crime against a minority) or a hurricane hits and that despair is revealed for the world to see."

Hundreds of listeners in the audience sat in sobering silence as Obama continued to speak. He then began to describe a future we all could aspire to. He talked about how we all had the power to "take the bullets out" of our society. He then asserted, "If we have more black men in prison than are in our colleges and universities, then it's time to take the bullet out. If we have almost two million people going to the emergency room for treatable illnesses like asthma that costs us half a billion dollars, it's time to take the bullet out. If one out of every nine kids doesn't have health insurance, it's time to take the bullet out. If we keep sending our kids to dilapidated school buildings, if we keep fighting this war in Iraq—a war that never should have been authorized and waged, a war that's costing us 275 million dollars a day, and the sacrifice of so many innocent lives—if we have all these challenges and nothing's changing, then every mayor in America needs to come together—form our surgery teams—and take the bullets out."[5]

Barack Obama went on to win the presidency of the United States eighteen months later. He served two terms as America's first Black president. He did so by appealing to the hopes and aspirations of all of the people of America. The self-described "skinny guy with a funny name" planted seeds of hope when he was an obscure junior senator from Illinois during the Democratic National Convention of 2004. He proclaimed in his fiery speech promoting John Kerry for President that America is "not liberal America or conservative America, it's the United States of America." He went on to say, "There's no Black America, or White America, or Latino America, or Asian America; there's the United States of America." His powerful words still ring true. I believe that despite anyone's specific political persuasion, it's really difficult to deny the positivity that President Obama infused into American politics.

5 Barack Obama, Remarks to the National Conference of Black Mayors in Baton Rouge, Louisiana Online by Gerhard Peters and John T. Woolley, The American Presidency Project

The vision of a brighter tomorrow has the power to inspire today and instill it with unstoppable energy.

What is your picture of tomorrow? Does it inspire you to dream or cause you nightmares? When you look into your "Abrahamic skies," are you able to see your stars of possibilities? When you look into your future, do you see a bullet excised? Your affirmative answers to these questions will determine the energy with which you approach today as we look into tomorrow for inspiration.

FOUR IMPORTANT PERSPECTIVES ABOUT TOMORROW

I have learned that perspective is everything. I have learned that "Whether you think you can, or you think you can't—you're right," like the famous Henry Ford once said. Therefore, I'd like to share with you four perspectives of tomorrow that I see as important to living today effectively.

- **Tomorrow cannot be lived today.** It's not that tomorrow is unimportant. It's just that we cannot live tomorrow today. Remember, if the fight is tomorrow, we cannot go around with a clenched fist today.

Congressman John Lewis was only twenty-three years old when he volunteered to help organize the famous March for Freedom and Jobs in Washington D.C., on August 28, 1963. The march where Martin Luther King, Jr. seized the historical moment and shared his "I Have a Dream" speech. John was also invited to speak. He was introduced as "young John Lewis, the student chairman of the Nonviolent Coordinating Committee." He recalled seeing hundreds of thousands of people on his left and people who climbed trees to get a better view of the speakers on his right. Young, passionate, and even militant, John recalled that he wrote a speech filled with words like "revolution" and threatening that if things didn't change, people would resort to drastic, violent measures. When Dr. King saw his speech, he advised John to soften the language a bit. John recalls that he did not want to—his fists were clenched for tomorrow's fight, he was filled with passion and anger, and he was ready for the fight. However, his love, respect, and admiration for his hero, Dr. King, were so great that he agreed to soften the language but keep the intent. John Lewis went on to fight many fights, living a long and notable life devoted to racial justice and civil rights. Mr. Lewis famously quipped in a debate that voters should send "a tugboat to Congress, not a showboat." The son of sharecroppers who finally saved enough to purchase their farm, John knew that progress entailed a marathon, not a sprint. Dr. King planted a seed of reflection in young, angry John Lewis, changing the course of his actions that day. John would devote his entire life to transforming the world and creating racial equality and became known as the Conscience of Congress.[6] He learned that tomorrow cannot be lived today.

6 *The March On Washington: John Lewis's Speech* (video) | MLK | TIME January 17, 2017

- **Tomorrow represents possibilities.** Tomorrow is a picture of the highest possibilities. Remember the story of Abraham. He was promised offspring as numerous as the starry host of the heavens. He believed in the incredible and received the impossible. We should live based on our best picture of tomorrow so that we can act on our dreams today.

President Abraham Lincoln faced consistent adversity throughout his life and his presidency. His difficulties started early in life. He grew up in poverty, and his mother died when he was just nine years old. He had a difficult relationship with his father. Soon after his mother's death, his father married Sarah Bush Johnston. In a time of great difficulty for young Abraham, the new Mrs. Lincoln showed him deep and unconditional love. She called Abraham "a model child who never needed a crossword." They had such a deep loving connection that she recalled that her mind and his mind "seemed to run together." President Lincoln would later visit his stepmother for the last time in early 1861, just before he left for Washington, D.C., to take the presidential oath. To friends accompanying him during his travels, Lincoln spoke very affectionately of his stepmother, calling her "the best friend" he'd ever had and recalling the positive impact she'd had on his life. Mrs. Lincoln planted a seed of affirmative possibility in a young, awkward boy who would become an admired and respected leader beyond his lifetime and around the world.[7]

---

7 Phillips, Donald T. 1992, *Lincoln on Leadership, Executive Strategies for Tough Times*, D.T.B. Companion Books, Illinois, USA

- **Tomorrow represents a harvest whose seed must be planted today.** Our understanding of tomorrow should encompass the ability to see the potential apple orchard in the tiny apple seed today. The possibility of tomorrow should unleash the potential in today. We must understand that just as every harvest is housed in a seed, so is tomorrow contained in a seed. Today is tomorrow concealed. Tomorrow is today's potential revealed. The ability for you to see that the harvest of tomorrow inside the seed of today is the key to effective living. We cannot live tomorrow today. We can only sow the seeds of tomorrow's harvest today, which is why it is so important we do not waste whatever we are given today.

I learned this lesson quite literally growing up on my grandfather's farm in Cameroon in central Africa. My grandfather didn't start as a farmer. He was originally a registered nurse. He had the unfortunate experience of receiving an incorrectly administered injection to the nerve, which resulted in a neurological disorder. He spent the rest of his life struggling with this neurological malfunction that cost him his professional nursing career. My grandfather dealt with the adversity of his life by changing careers and becoming a farmer. He planted an orchard that would become one of the hallmarks of his life. Because of my grandfather's ability to let go of his yesterday and embrace the *today* before him, the local villagers became interested in progressing beyond the typical subsistence farming into more lucrative agriculture.

As a five-year-old growing up with my grandparents, I couldn't help but learn important agricultural concepts that have stayed with me for a lifetime. These lessons have served as a metaphor for all that can happen in life. My grandpa taught me to cultivate guava, mangos, plums, avocado, pineapples, bananas, and coffee, among other fruit trees. As early as the age of five, I could appreciate the power and potential of a seed. Each season after harvest, Grandpa would have all of the children select the best seed of every kind of fruit tree in the orchard for re-planting in the future. I observed a planted bean seed unleash its tender shoot—pushing aside the dirt and little rocks— to make its way through the fallow ground and rise to embrace the sunlight. I had observed how my grandfather, from one guava seed, grew the largest guava orchard in my little village. Life's adversity planted a seed in my grandfather that helped him to embrace the possibility before him to be a role model to an entire village. The seed he planted allowed his grandson to deeply understand the power of potential and take that wisdom with him throughout his entire life. Grandpa taught me that every seed is a potential orchard; and that the earlier we plant the seed, the sooner we can expect the orchard.

- **Use tomorrow's hope to inspire today.** I will never forget how I felt listening to Presidential Candidate Obama on that fateful day in May 2007. I was one of the many who thronged to the front to meet and greet him and to take a photo with him. I remember going home later that day and just feeling like my future was possible. Hope inspires, friends! In all of your losing, never lose hope. It is an energy generator. It's the dynamo of a productive life.

When President Barack Obama was inaugurated as the forty-fourth President of the United States and the first African American President in United States history, Congressman John Lewis stood nearby. After the ceremony was complete, John handed President Obama his program from the historic inauguration to autograph. It must've been an incredibly moving moment for John Lewis, a man who'd spent his entire life—even enduring vicious beatings—fighting racial injustice. The exchange took place in the same city where Dr. King advised young John Lewis to soften his words. President Obama autographed the program and handed it to Congressman Lewis. He wrote, "Because of you, John." The seed that John Lewis and a host of others had planted when he was a young man at the march in Washington in 1963 had resulted in the historic harvest of the first Black president.

What does tomorrow mean to *you*? Do you see possibilities or impossibilities? Hope or despair? Dreams or nightmares?

Our ability to see tomorrow in terms of the possibility of our hopes and dreams is critical to igniting inspiration in the present moment to propel us forward.

TAKE YOUR TURN:
HOW CAN YOU MAKE TODAY COUNT?

1. What is your big picture of Tomorrow?

_____

_____

_____

_____

_____

_____

_____

2. What would your life look like today if you lived it with the inspiration of tomorrow's dreams?

_____

_____

_____

_____

_____

_____

_____

3. What picture of the future *inspires* you the most (please, take time and write them down):

• In your personal life

_____

_____

_____

• In your family/relational life

_____

_____

_____

• In your career life

_____

_____

_____

• In your business/professional life

_____

_____

_____

4. What action(s) are you willing to take today based on the possibilities of tomorrow's dreams?

_____

_____

_____

_____

_____

_____

_____

CHAPTER 5

LOOK BACKWARD FOR EDUCATION

"I never lose, I only win or I learn."

Nelson Mandela (1918-2013)
President of South Africa, Anti-apartheid Revolutionary

Alan Paton (1903–1988) was a South African writer and anti-apartheid activist. In his most celebrated work, *Cry, the Beloved Country*, Alan Paton provides a profound insight into what it means to look back into our life experiences for education.

Alan Paton's world-renowned novel, *Cry, the Beloved Country*, was published in 1948 in the United States by Charles Scribner's Sons and in London by Jonathon Cape. The novel became an instant bestseller worldwide upon its release. This piece was later turned into two films of the same name, produced in 1951 and 1995.

The popularity of the book, I believe, derives from a core message that resonated with many. The book tells the painful story of the son of a Black Anglican priest who unintentionally kills Arthur Jarvis, the son of a prominent white, wealthy landowner. Arthur was known as a kind man and a passionate advocate for social justice, devoting his whole life to attempting to right the wrongs of the apartheid system, even though he was born into wealth and privilege. His father was distant from the problems of society, while he notably benefitted from the mistreatment of others.

Arthur's killer would later be discovered as Reverend Kumalo's son, Absalom, who left his home in the small village of Ndotsheni to work in the sordid, dangerous city of Johannesburg. Absalom worked in a factory, gambled, spent some time in a reformatory, and ultimately impregnated a local girl. Reverend Kumalo knew none of this when he was called to go to the city to assist his sister, who he learned was in trouble. Reverend Kumalo traveled to Johannesburg at great personal risk and expense to find and help his sister, Gertrude. Once he arrived, he painfully learned she had turned to prostitution and selling alcohol to support herself and her young son. At this point, Reverend Kumalo had no idea of the life his son was leading. He only knew that he had not seen his son in a very long time and that he should not waste the opportunity given him in the present moment to connect with his son, Absalom.

Reverend Kumalo's brother, Joseph, had left his village long ago to make his life in Johannesburg, becoming a wealthy businessman and politician. He abandoned the knowledge and the wisdom of the Zulu people to fully embrace and support Western ways of thinking and working. Before moving to Johannesburg, Joseph was a humble carpenter. Reverend Kumalo took the opportunity to reconnect with his brother, intending to seek his brother's assistance in finding Absalom. As he searched for his son, Reverend Kumalo witnessed the devastation of extreme poverty and segregation of daily life in South Africa. During his search, he learned the tragic news that the white liberal activist Arthur Jarvis had been accidentally murdered during a robbery attempt by three Black men. He'd come to find out that it was his son, Absalom, who pulled the trigger.

James Jarvis received the crushing news of his son's murder while tending to his palatial estate. He rushed to Johannesburg, leaving his wife and young son behind. He had no idea that he was riding the same train, in segregated cars, as the father of his son's murderer. Absalom was ironically defended, in court, by an attorney *pro deo* (for God). Absalom confessed to the murder, truthfully telling the judge he was scared and the shooting was unintentional. The other two men were released; however, Absalom was charged for the murder and hanged. The two fathers built an unlikely, tentative friendship, with the wealthy Jarvis making small donations to help the village. He was inspired by his younger son, who continually reached out to help the people in the village. Ultimately, the broken-hearted fathers meet on the vast, unspeakably beautiful land bound by their tragic grief. James Jarvis, stricken with the awareness that his life contributed to the tragedy, agrees to help Reverend Kumalo build a church.

Cry, the Beloved Country was banned in South Africa due to its potentially politically dangerous material. The nation's leadership was not willing or ready to confront the lessons of the painful and tortuous segregation system. All this happened while the rest of the world was fascinated by this inspirational story. *Cry, the Beloved Country* went on to sell fifteen million copies during Alan Paton's lifetime. Paton died in 1988, never living to see the abolishment of apartheid in 1994.

As of this writing, we are in the midst of two major world events. We continue to manage the effects of the COVID-19 pandemic and are also experiencing unprecedented racial unrest and growing awareness of racial inequities. Martin Luther King, Jr. wisely advised us, "Injustice anywhere is a threat to justice everywhere." Unfortunately, we still have a long way to go in the healing of the wounds of racial injustice. It is worth noting that, in addition to the pandemic, there have been protests in the United States and around the world in reaction to the deaths of unarmed Black men and women at the hands of police officers. This disturbing systemic trend has opened up a national—and even global—discussion on racial injustice, white privilege, and racial reconciliation.

It is obvious that the wounds of the past have not been adequately addressed. To move forward, we cannot only count our blessings; we must count our lessons too! In a short time, we forgot the lessons of the past. It was Alan

Paton who said, "It's not 'forgive and forget' as if nothing ever happened. It's 'forgive and go forward,' building on the mistakes of the past and the energy generated by thoughtful reconciliation to create a new future." Wisdom demands we learn from the painful past if we do not want to repeat this past again and again.

I remember listening to a teaching by one of my mentors at the beginning of the COVID-19 pandemic. In his talk, he related how tragedies like pandemics eventually do pass away and how what endures depends on what we do or refuse to do in these moments.

Hence, I resolved in March of 2020, when we did not know the full extent of the severity of the impact of the COVID-19 pandemic, that I would not let it deter me from my goals and plans for 2020. I was planning a conference which was intended to be held in Africa. The pandemic forced me to redirect and create a virtual conference. I initially anticipated that guests from five countries would attend the conference in person. Through the blessing of technology and the seeming adversity of the pandemic, my team and I were able to reach over one thousand attendees from *sixty countries*, including Cameroon, South Africa, Nigeria, Ghana, Sebago, the Congo, Belgium, France, China, and the United States. Moreover, we had several dozen people sign up for our mentorship program to enable them to become change leaders in their communities and nations around the world. The past has taught us that tragedy does pass away, but what we do during these moments can outlive our lifetimes. The key is to learn from the past!

Had I been limited to my original idea of what the conference would be like, I never would have entertained all of the options and possibilities of holding the conference online. If I did not look to the future, I could've been sitting in an empty room with very few people. Instead, this new method of reaching people allowed me and my team to plant more seeds than we had ever thought possible just a year before.

Reflection pushes us to be open to a greater perspective and possibilities because clearly, possibilities exist even when we can't see them. We use but a fraction of our potential. Wherever God places us, we can excel, even amid a pandemic. The conference turned out to be the most rewarding conference in the last several years. Who could have ever believed it? The year 2020 has been amazing in so many ways.

The concept of looking backward for education tells us that "experience is not the best teacher; experience reflected upon is the best teacher," as my mentor John Maxwell has put it. Insight from experience and lessons learned from experience become our best teachers.

If you fail a thousand times and continue to fail the same way, you haven't learned anything. We must look at the past from a reflective point of view. If the past has a positive experience, we must find a way to make these experiences a repeat occurrence. We must all seek to make positive experiences a constant theme in our lives today.

History clearly shows that learning from experience is no easy task. It is effortless to review societal actions and confidently point out where the world is failing; however, it is challenging to deeply review our pasts to learn from circumstances and experiences to build a more productive future.

I have formulated a plan that allows individuals to use yesterday's experience, whatever it might be so that it can become a benchmark for a future positive experience. It is possible to limit a bad experience to yesterday and eliminate the risk that it will creep into your today. There are readily identifiable thoughts that continually ruin lives. There are tools anyone can use to help limit yesterday and ensure that past circumstances will not have an impact on the future. It is very possible to contain the negative past, keep it in the past, and not allow it to encroach into today so that it will not negatively impact tomorrow.

Through my research, life experience, teaching, and continual study, I have noted there are warning signs that we can all take charge of once we are aware of them. I have summarized them into five categories of behaviors you may recognize in yourself and others.

FIVE TYPES OF PEOPLE IN THE WORLD

There are five broad categories of people based on their perspective of yesterday. Interestingly, I have found that the lessons learned from these different vantage points can be both positive and negative. Nonetheless, each perspective is important because it can increase our understanding of people's actions today based on yesterday.

It's been said that "perspective is everything." Whether we believe that the world is loving and kind or we believe that the world is wicked and treacherous may not change the world, but it shapes our world. Our worldview will influence our behavior and how we interact with others.

The recent societal events of racial unrest and reactions to the pandemic easily remind me of all of the lessons that history has taught us, whether it be examples from apartheid South Africa, as exemplified in the Alan Paton story, or our own experiences.

For instance, at the time of writing this chapter, the COVID-19 virus has claimed over two hundred thousand lives in the United States of America alone. People are still struggling with what to make of this human tragedy.

The following section details five categories of individuals based on their perspective of yesterday.

Lesson 1: People who have learned nothing from their past are *Repeaters* of history.

> *"Those who cannot remember the past are condemned to repeat it."*

George Santayana, (1863-1952)
Spanish-American philosopher

One would think that after losing over two hundred thousand human lives in a pandemic, everyone would live a rather reasonably cautious life. But as news reports have shown, as soon as the economy began to show signs of recovery, many people began to engage in social activities as if all was back to normal and the risks had dissolved. Large crowds of people gathered, without wearing masks, and without acknowledging social distancing. This disregard for the health advisory caused a relapse of the pandemic in particular regions and states throughout the country. The *Repeaters* refused to learn from history, and history repeated itself.

The other timely example we are currently addressing is the mass protests and riots occurring in the United States, decrying what some perceive as systemic injustices. Some people choose to unilaterally condemn the protests and riots, without acknowledging the pain and frustration causing the outburst. The *Repeaters* will not evaluate the past to attempt to address the root cause of the crisis.

As stated earlier, Martin Luther King, Jr. observed in his *Letters from the Birmingham Jail*, "Injustice anywhere is a threat to justice everywhere." He continued to write, "We are caught in an inescapable network of mutuality, tied in a single garment of destiny." Those words ring so true today. Once again, people have unfortunately forgotten that injustice begets injustice. They have forgotten that when we accept the violation of others' rights somewhere, we are tolerating the violation of rights elsewhere! Summarily, we have not learned from the past if we do not solve the problem of injustice but still expect to live peaceable lives.

There are an awful lot of people who cause history to repeat again and again in life, business, and the workplace because of this stubborn refusal to learn from history.

Are you a *Repeater* of history?

Lesson 2: People who run from their past are *Escapists*.

"The past can hurt. But the way I see it, you can either run from it or learn from it."

Walt Disney (1901-1966)
American entrepreneur, animator, writer,
voice actor, and film producer

The truth is some people have made a reputation of running from their past. They want to numb the hurt. They cannot stand the pain. However, in the end, they only postpone their hurt and pain.

Escapists are similar to addicts. They do not like the pain. They do not want the hurt. So they indulge in a drug to make the pain go away. They shut down the pain. But as soon as the substance disappears, their problems reappear. They are again triggered. And the endless cycle begins. *Escapists* believe that if they run far enough from the past and deny it long enough, they will finally be free from it. Nothing can be farther from the truth!

The pandemic, again, serves as a good example to demonstrate how *Escapists* cope. I have noticed people who have decided to live a "normal" life as though the pandemic never happened. It is as though they want to deny or ignore the existence of the virus. However, the reality is that, in the foreseeable future, we are going to live with the virus for some time. Ignoring or denying this truth will not and cannot help us.

By the same token, if we do not take steps to solve the current racial tensions, protests and riots will continue around the country. The United States has an unacknowledged past, a past that is not pretty or rosy—a past that viewed Black people as being less than human. We must acknowledge that it was wrong then and that it is still wrong now. We all must rise as a people and fix it. No denying this reality will help us.

Are you running from your past? Are you afraid to face it? Don't be an *Escapist*! Take this moment in time and confront it.

Look directly into the face of your yesterday. Accept it and deal with it.

Lesson 3: People who try to erase rather than embrace their past are *Revisionists*.

> *"Never erase your past. It shapes who you are today and will help you to be the person you'll be tomorrow."*
>
> Ziad Abdelnour (1960-present)
> President & CEO, Blackhawk Partners Inc.

I say, don't try to erase the past; rather, embrace it!

The Holocaust was a dark time in history. It is often used to describe the period in Nazi Germany between 1933 and 1945 when, under the leadership of Adolf Hitler, the anti-Semitic regime persecuted and killed Jews, whom they viewed as being an inferior race. Approximately six million Jews were killed, while five million others were also targeted (for racial, political, ideological, and behavioral reasons) and killed.[8] To this date, there are a host of individuals—and entire nations—who still believe that horrific historic event never happened or was not nearly what it is said to be.

Revisionists of this part of history either delete this historical fact or rewrite it to make it less serious. In

---

8 "Documenting Numbers of Victims of the Holocaust & Nazi Persecution." U.S. Holocaust Museum accessed 9/23/2020

much the same way, many people try to rewrite the past they do not want to live with by stating a narrative they are comfortable with to move ahead. However, the recipe for a clean conscience today is not erasing the past but embracing it.

I am not saying that by embracing the past, we should celebrate the past. I am saying that we must acknowledge it for its merits and, if we find it disturbing, make a conscious decision to correct its mistakes.

Have you ever tried to erase portions of your life that make you uncomfortable? Do you struggle with embracing the "not-so-good aspects" of your past life? One way of dealing with that past is to come to terms with the truth that *it happened*. It may make you cry. It might make you sad. It might make you angry with yourself or with others. All of those reactions are fine.

Embracing the past is a courageous act. This might be a good place to pause and seek help if it is needed. Permit yourself to do so. Please, use the link www. thedaybeforetomrorrow.store/help to seek help if necessary; it is only human. There is no need for shame. We all deserve to lead a happy and peaceful life. The resource is there for you now or whenever you are ready.

The only way to walk past your past is to acknowledge it in the first place. Embrace your past today.

Lesson 4: People who live in the past are *Nostalgics*.

*"You do not move ahead by constantly looking
in a rearview mirror. The past is a rudder to
guide you, not an anchor to drag you. We must
learn from the past but not live in the past."*

Warren Wiersbe (1929-2019)
Pastor and author of fifty books known as the *Be* series)

Do you remember the tale of two brothers that I told you
about in chapter 2? Greg and Jeff had the same past. They
were both raised by a troubled father. Greg turned out to be
a physician, philanthropist, family man, and a community
favorite. Jeff, on the other hand, became a high-school
dropout, an addict, a felon, and suffered poor health.

Upon examining Jeff's story, I soon noticed that he
inherited his father's addictions and harmful lifestyle at a
young age. And though he would have chance after chance
in and out of jail, he just didn't make it to wholesomeness.
One characteristic defense he had was repeating the story
to himself and others of what his father did to him. He'd
state, "See what my father did to me? The abuse, the
neglect, and the poor example he set? How could I become
anything better?"

Remember, though, that his brother, Greg,
went through the same abuse and poor upbringing.
Nevertheless, these two ended up with two entirely
different destinies. Without making light of the difficult

struggles and challenges these two brothers underwent, it seems clear that Jeff ended up stuck in his past.

He was stuck with the memories of abuse he would not let go of. He did not overcome the poor self-esteem he struggled with. Feeling worthless had become a common theme in his life. The pain was real, the blame palpable, and the suffering debilitating. However, he stayed there. He toiled in that dark space and would stay there for almost a lifetime.

It is a sad truth, but many live in the past. It's familiar territory. It's like the devil we know. The future is fearful. It is an unknown. The future is like an angel we do not know. We, unfortunately, prefer the familiar past rather than risk losing what is not working for us to accept an unknown future.

There is hope. You can learn from the past. You can learn to enjoy working in the present toward a future that is brighter than you currently think is possible.

In all of your living, do not live in the past!

Lesson 5: People who have learned from the past are *Futurists*.

> *"The illiterate of the 21t century will not be those who cannot read and write, but those who cannot learn, unlearn, and relearn."*

Alvin Toffler (1928-1926)
Author, businessman, and futurist

I have learned that for people to focus on today and create a better future, they must learn from their past. The ability to acquire education from life experiences and the past is critical for future success.

I'd like to bring you back to the story of the news of the unfolding pandemic and how it affected my plans for 2020, especially the two conferences I committed to lead. I remember vividly when the COVID-19 pandemic hit the United States. State after state was forced to shut down their respective economies and public life. I belong to an association of coaches and speakers called the John Maxwell Team. Our annual spring conference was due in March of that year. However, because of the national and international travel shutdowns, the conference organizers were forced to cancel the conference.

Given the uncertainty that loomed, the founder of the John Maxwell Team, Mr. John Maxwell, held a series of teaching meetings called "Leading Through a Crisis." One of the central tenets of these teachings was to help our tens of thousands of coaches and speakers look at the pandemic in the light of past alarming situations and to draw lessons from them.

There was a particular emphasis on seeking to pivot to the opportunities and advantages that could present themselves amid the challenge. I remember deciding then that I was going to grow myself and my team to not only survive but also thrive in the pandemic. I made a particular resolve to write this book, to connect in greater ways with my family, to grow my business, and to seek every opportunity possible to serve the needy in my community and the world.

As the pandemic progressed, the picture seemed increasingly grim. It was not evident how thriving during this challenging time would happen. Not knowing how things would turn out, I began taking steps toward my goal. I started by hosting teaching lessons on how to thrive in a pandemic. Then I got the opportunity to join my church family in hosting two *Feeding America* events. What I did not see coming was how the two annual conferences I organized through one of my organizations would turn out.

LEAD Missions International is an organization I founded to teach and train leaders around the world, especially leaders from developing countries. We had planned four conference events for July of 2020 in Yaoundé, Cameroon, Central Africa. When it was clear the pandemic was not letting up, we decided to move the conferences to August. Even so, the pandemic prevailed. Just sixty days before the scheduled event dates, we decided to hold our two conferences entirely online, something we were not quite sure how to do.

This was when we experienced the advantage in the adversity. Instead of a few nations participating—

typically five—we had registrations from over a thousand participants from sixty nations across the world. This was simply unbelievable! It made me believe that adversity is the womb of opportunity.

It all began with John Maxwell's lesson, with the seed he planted on having the right perspective in a crisis. Looking back at lessons learned from previous global crises, my team was able to not only survive in a challenging time but also break records in our outreach efforts.

Marianne Williamson, author, spiritual leader, politician, and activist, advises, "Whatever worked in the past, build on it; whatever didn't work in the past, break the chain that binds you to it."

We can use the past as an important vehicle to drive us into our future. As Gianni Versace, the Italian fashion designer, commented, "I am not interested in the past, except as the road to the future."

We must see the past as a conduit to our future— not an anchor.

CONCLUSION

In conclusion, I have found the following words to be both instructive and insightful. Yes, we can look to the past for education.

"The past is behind; learn from it. The future is ahead; prepare for it. The present is here; live it."

Thomas Monson (1927-2018)
Sixteenth President of the Church of Latter-Day Saints

TAKE YOUR TURN:
HOW CAN YOU MAKE TODAY COUNT?

1. What is your overall memory of yesterday? Do you find a situation repeating in your life? Are you attracting a certain type of person or finding yourself in a similar situation? Are you having the same argument? What is it? How could it be different from the lessons learned from yesterday?

_____

_____

_____

_____

_____

_____

2. What would your life look like today if your significant memories of yesterday became your most important lessons of today?

_____

_____

_____

_____

_____

_____

Regarding your perspective of yesterday, what personality type are you—a *Repeater*, an *Escapist*, a *Revisionist*, a *Nostalgic*, or a *Futurist*? How have you grown? How has your perspective changed? What needs work?

• In your personal life

_____

_____

_____

_____

_____

• In your family/relational life

_____

_____

_____

_____

_____

• In your career life

_____

_____

_____

_____

_____

• In your business/professional life

_____

_____

_____

_____

_____

3. What action(s) are you willing to take today based on the lessons of yesterday to create a better tomorrow?

_____

_____

_____

_____

_____

_____

_____

CHAPTER 6

PUT A DEMAND ON TODAY

"If I waste today, I destroy the last page of my life.
Therefore, each hour of this day will I cherish
for it can never return."

Og Mandino,
American author (1923-1996)

MY STORY

As a young immigrant who arrived in the United States
of America with just six hundred dollars to my name, I
learned in a fresh new way what it means to "live a day at a
time." Although I did not notice this at the time, the mantra
is true regardless of a person's financial status or mental
state of being. I have the unique ability to share this truth
from the perspective of a position of poverty as well as
from someone who has created financial success. It is only
possible to live life one day at a time. While we are at it, we
must live life to the fullest potential possible every day.

When I arrived in the United States, I had no idea
how I was going to pay for my graduate studies. The
university I attended had an uncommon policy. As long as
students were able to pay a portion of their tuition, they

were allowed to stay in classes. There was a condition, however, that the classes must be paid in full before the student could continue to the next semester. I focused on my dream of pursuing my university education by fiercely concentrating on my studies. I was on my way. My grades were excellent. When a friend learned of my financial situation, he agreed to loan me a thousand dollars. Even with the loan, I still did not have enough money to pay for all of my tuition. When it was time to register for the next semester, I had an outstanding balance.

I faced additional financial obstacles. As an international student, I was not eligible for financial aid and didn't even qualify to apply for student loans. I was allowed to work. However, there were limitations here too. I was limited to working on the university campus. I was attending school in New Orleans in 2007, two years after Hurricane Katrina had struck. There was still significant recovery clean-up to do. Some houses needed to be gutted, and debris needed to be removed from the surrounding area. It was informal work, and I helped a couple of families for a daily appreciation rate of about a hundred dollars, not nearly enough to pay for the tuition. I was faced with the choice of sitting at home with zero dollars, worrying about my situation, or getting up to go do the backbreaking work of moving heavy furniture to storage facilities, knowing it would bring me closer to my goal.

When I'm at similar crossroads in my life, I evaluate

what the cost of doing something is versus the cost of doing nothing. I found time to do the work on weekends while studying and attending classes during the week. I took the low-paying work because it needed to be done, and I was available to do it. I knew the seed of the money would grow and one day help me to achieve my goals.

My professors would sometimes be perplexed when I wasn't registered for the next semester. They would notice that my name was not on the list of registered students. They would advise that I speak to the registrar, certain that my name was omitted from the list of continuing students by error. Sharing the truth with them required some humility. It was humiliating for me to tell them the same story semester after semester about my situation. I wanted desperately to continue my studies and solve my financial issues. I would do all I could to stay enrolled.

I was surrounded by professors and students who believed in me and recognized my dream. They felt almost compelled to step in and help me if they could. Throughout my graduate school tenure, three professors and two students loaned me the money on the condition that I would pay it back, and thankfully, I did. As a result of trusting them enough to tell the truth, they were willing to help me. I approached each semester this way, focusing on my intention, knowing that it would work out if only I continued to do the best I could in every way—by studying, working where I could, and connecting with people who would be willing to support my dream. That's the story of how I paid for my graduate degrees. Taking one semester at a time, doing what I could do to satisfy the requirements, and focusing on my goal of achieving my graduate education.

Even when people have a lot of resources, they still must live one day at a time. Of course, they won't have to worry about paying their basic living expenses or for the things they need. They still have the opportunity to embrace each day with its limitless possibilities but with a different set of challenges. They may be relational, emotional, mental, or attitudinal. Or the challenge might just be understanding how to use their resources wisely. The professors and students who loaned me money were not that rich. However, they had more funds than I did at the time, and they believed in me. They were willing to put action to their generosity. Their faith in me allowed me to finish my studies, become a university professor, start three separate businesses, and write a book to share my story. The seeds of kindness they planted have enabled me not only to become the person I am but to travel the world and meet influential people of all stripes—from presidents to peasants, businessmen to congressmen, laymen to the clergy; it has been a rewarding experience I will never forget. We all have the power to grasp the potential of today, no matter what our status is in life.

LIVE LIFE TO THE FULLEST

I also learned an important principle from one of my favorite authors, motivational speakers, and leadership experts of all time, Dr. Myles Munroe. This great leader lost his life in a tragic plane crash in his homeland in the Bahamas in September 2014. In his life's work, he taught the all-important principle of living life to the fullest and dying empty.

Dr. Munroe taught the following:

> The wealthiest place in the world is not the gold mines of South America or the oil fields of Iraq or Iran. They are not the diamond mines of South Africa or the banks of the world. The wealthiest place on the planet is just down the road. It is the cemetery. There lie buried companies that were never started, inventions that were never made, bestselling books that were never written, and masterpieces that were never painted. In the cemetery is buried the greatest treasure of untapped potential.
>
> Dr. Munroe

I remember listening to Dr. Munroe when I was a freshman in college say, "The greatest tragedy in life is not death, but a life without a purpose." This thought was profound to me. It began to shape my life and thoughts as a young college student about the importance of purposeful living. Hearing Dr. Munroe's words inspired me to develop a plan for how to avoid enriching the cemetery with unfinished purpose and untapped potential. I remember praying in my university room, *Oh Lord, I do not want to die taking my dreams to the grave. I do not want to live an unfulfilled life. I do not want to die with untapped potential. Let me die empty!*

In hindsight, I believe this prayer was answered. I believe it is still being answered today. In the past several years, I have benefited from the understanding of becoming intentional about my life. I live with the consciousness that each day is a gift to be unwrapped and used to the maximum. I have learned that each day comes pregnant with a purpose that can be maximized beyond our imagination. I have come to understand that each day comes loaded with intentions that need to be mobilized for the good of humanity and the preservation of mankind. Through the benefit of my struggles and the uncertainty that I have faced, I have learned the ability to put a demand on today. To live each day doing the best I can is one of the most rewarding things I have learned. I believe we all can put a demand on our day to deliver for us no matter what.

DON'T PLAY SMALL

Nelson Mandela, former political prisoner and president of South Africa, once said, "There is no passion to be found playing small—in settling for a life that is less than the one you are capable of living."

I agree with his wisdom and have created this mantra for my life: "Do not leave today standing in the presence of your absence." Be present in your present. Show up for this day that has shown up for you. Lay hold on to this day that has been given to you.

Realizing that knowledge alone and understanding will not maximize the potential of tomorrow, people need to *do* something. Demand requires action. Demand action on today from yourself. Decide you will not accept anything less than today's true worth.

When we begin to grasp the profound reality of the worth of today, we can better understand the possibility of tomorrow and the lessons of tomorrow. We might gaze far off into the horizon, envisioning the picture of tomorrow's harvest. We thoughtfully embrace the lessons of yesterday, understanding that yesterday is gone forever. Once we accept these substantial truths, we begin to understand how critical the intersection of today is.

You must put pressure on today to release the best possible life that is available to you.

FIVE KEYS TO MAXIMIZING TODAY

I have learned from personal experience and great achievers that there are five keys to maximizing today.

1.   **Today is all you have. Live it as if it was your last.**

> *"If today were the last day of my life, would I want to do what I'm about to do today? Whenever the answer has been 'no' for too many days in a row, I know I need to change something."*

Steve Jobs
CEO and Cofounder of Apple Computers
and Pixar Animation Studios

Steve Jobs discusses the unusual path of his life in the commencement speech he gave to the graduates of Stanford University in 2005. Steve shared with this esteemed group of graduates that he was a college dropout. He went on to share that his biological mother was an unmarried graduate student who gave him up for adoption. She felt very strongly that her child should receive a college education. A lawyer and his wife agreed to adopt the child at birth. When Steve arrived, the couple decided at the last minute that they wanted a girl. Steve's parents, a working-class couple with no formal education, were on a waiting list, hoping to adopt a child. They received a call that a baby was available. Without hesitation, they agreed to welcome the child into their home and begin their family. When the biological mother learned that the adoptive mother never finished college and the adoptive father didn't even finish high school, she refused to sign the adoption papers. She only reluctantly agreed to give the baby up for adoption on the condition that the adoptive parents would commit to providing a college education to the infant. They agreed.

When Steve was old enough to go to college, he naively chose Reed College, a very expensive school that required his parents to spend all of their savings on tuition. At a young age, he had no idea what he wanted to do with his life. Spending his parents' entire life savings without a purpose was tearing him up inside. Knowing attending college was the wrong decision for him, he decided to drop out after six months and trust that it would all work out okay. The minute Steve dropped out, he no longer had to take courses that didn't interest him. He was able to drop in on classes he was interested in.

At the time, Reed College offered one of the most advanced courses on the art of calligraphy. Every poster and every label on every drawer throughout the campus was beautifully hand-calligraphed. Since Steve was no longer bound by a curriculum, he decided to take a calligraphy class. He learned about the intricacy of typefaces and what makes great typography great. Steve noticed that the historical art form was beautiful and subtle in a way that science cannot capture. At the time, studying calligraphy didn't provide hope of any practical application in his life and likely seemed to be a waste of time.

Ten years later, when he was designing the first Macintosh computer, the benefit of the art of calligraphy came back to him. The Macintosh computer was the first computer with beautiful typography written into the software. Steve contended that if he had never dropped out of college and dropped into that single course, the Macintosh computer would have never had multiple typefaces and proportionately spaced fonts. All computer software now uses this elegant font design. If it were not for Steve Jobs saying 'no' to what was not right for him at the time, the world would be at a great artistic loss[9].

If today was the last day of your life, would you do what you are doing now?

2. Today is the battle day of your life. Make sure you win it.

This truth was demonstrated to me when I read a story of ten cancer survivors in 2016[10]. The common thread in their stories seemed to be that they perceived each day as a battle they had to face and win. Regardless of their age or their status in life, they seemed to grasp the possibilities that were before them. The following captures a few of the messages shared in the stories of hope.

When fifty-one-year-old Julie Genovesi learned she

---

9 Stanford YouTube Channel accessed 11/9/2020
10 December 20, 2016, 10 Powerful Survivor Stories from 2016, www.cancer.org accessed 11/9/2020

had lung cancer, she was in complete shock. Before her diagnosis, she was healthy, and she had never smoked a day in her life. Furthermore, she was a runner and worked out every day. Julie noted, "When you're staring at something like this, you have to make every moment count. That's the only way to get through it: day by day." It must have been a difficult shift for Julie to release the life she thought she had, to embrace the situation before her.

Sophia Anagnostou was just twelve years old and finishing sixth grade when she began experiencing shortness of breath, pain in her wrists, and headaches. She was soon diagnosed with leukemia. Young Sophia wisely shares that she "tries to live life to the fullest," adding that she is "grateful to be able to run and go outside and eat in restaurants." She adds that these were things she never really thought about before, but she is aware of how wonderful these abilities are and thinks about them now.

Forty-seven-year-old Chrissy Dunn states that her life was shattered when she received a terminal pancreatic cancer diagnosis in 2015. She defied the odds and is still alive to tell her story today. She shares that she has "learned to look at things as blessings" that she used to take for granted. She notes that she cherishes "the shoes on her feet, the hot water for a bath" and adds that "every single aspect" of life is a blessing.

These great truths are available to all of us every day. Today is a battle to be fought and won.

3. Take care of today, and you'll not have to worry about
    tomorrow.

Tomorrow's success begins today. Mahatma Gandhi,
Indian lawyer, anti-colonial activist, and political ethicist,
famously stated, "We must be the change we wish to see in
the world." He did so by capturing the opportunities that
were available to him at the moment. As a consequence, the
story of India can hardly be told without his mention.

When India was a British colony, the British Raj
imposed a severe tax on salt imports[11]. This tax affected
all Indians regardless of their wealth or social class.
The crippling tax gave the oppressive leader power over
millions of people. Gandhi implemented the peaceful
Salt March beginning on March 12, 1930, by organizing
seventy-nine of his trusted volunteers. With people
walking ten miles each day, the march spanned 240 miles
over twenty-five days. Growing numbers of Indians joined
them along the way, increasing the group size to over
fifty thousand marchers. Gandhi led the massive group
of people, and they made salt along the way through
evaporation. The march gained worldwide attention and
gave impetus to the Independence Movement. It is said
Dr. Martin Luther King, Jr. was inspired by this act of
nonviolent civil disobedience, thus shaping the civil rights
movement in the United States.

---

11 "Mass civil disobedience throughout India followed as millions broke salt
laws" from Dalton's introduction to Ghandi's *Civil Disobelience*, Ghandi and
Dalton, p. 72

Gandhi chose the commodity of salt on which to stage the protests. He knew salt was an item that was used daily and that all people relied on. Gandhi stated, "Next to air and water, salt is perhaps the greatest necessity of life."

By seizing the day and doing that which was necessary to be done, we can change not only today but forever impact tomorrow.

4. Do not leave for tomorrow what you can do today.

Bishop Rosie O'Neil once said, "Procrastination is the arrogant assumption that God owes you another chance to do tomorrow what he gave you the chance to do today."

Benjamin Franklin, one of the founding fathers of the United States, lived by this maxim. He was a writer, a printer, a political philosopher, a politician, a postmaster, a scientist, an inventor, a humorist, a civic activist, a statesman, and a diplomat. He is also known for stating, "Don't put off until tomorrow what you can do today." He certainly proved that with all of his life's great accomplishments.

5. Do *all* you can do today, and know that *all* is enough.

"Finish each day and be done with it. You have done what you could. Learn from it... tomorrow is a new day."

Ralph Waldo Emerson
Philosopher and Poet (1803-1882)

Arthur L. Williams, Jr. had a humble start in life. Williams' father died of a heart attack in 1965 when Mr. Williams was twenty-three years old. His father had a whole life insurance policy, a very popular financial instrument at the time, which unfortunately left the family without enough financial resources, despite his father's best efforts. When his father passed, Mr. Williams was fulfilling his dream of being a high school coach, earning a moderate wage of $10,700 per year. In 1970, his cousin introduced him to the concept of term life insurance, a much less expensive option than whole life insurance. Most people didn't even know such a policy existed. Mr. Williams' father certainly didn't.

Arthur Williams continued to learn about insurance policies. He could find no adequate reason why the policies were not being marketed to the vast amounts of people and families who would benefit from them. Williams and his cousin went to work for an insurance company. They learned all about the intricacies of the insurance policies available to people and realized there were millions of people who could benefit from this knowledge. In 1997, the cousins founded their own company, A.L. Williams & Associates. They started with eighty-five insurance agents, and the company eventually grew to become Primerica Insurance.

Mr. Williams used a personal touch with his agents, knowing that communicating with them individually would make a difference in how they communicated with their customers. Before anyone was embracing video technology, he established weekly broadcast meetings on a private television broadcast system owned by the company. Using this method, he was able to individually connect with over a hundred thousand agents, ensuring they would stick to the company's philosophy of delivering financial services to the people that needed them with unwavering integrity. Mr. Williams attributes the growth of his company, which became the largest seller of life insurance in the United States, to promote his people. I agree with him and see evidence of the seeds of opportunity he planted within each of the insurance agents[12].

Mr. Williams once said, "All you can do is all you can do. But all you can do is enough." We can and should live life doing all that needs to be done today. But we can also live with the understanding that if we can do *all* we need to, all is enough!

These well-known heroes and everyday people demonstrate that we can live our best lives by putting a demand on today regardless of what our circumstances are. One person's gifts and opportunities are not greater than another's. By learning from the past and having a dream for the future, we can maximize the use of today. None of us has a clue about how living each day to the fullest can benefit mankind. Live today to the fullest, and do not squander the *present*.

12 Williams, Art with Hutto Kassel, Karen, 2013, *Coach, The A. L. Williams Story. How a no-name company led by a football coach, revolutionized the Life Insurance Industry.* Nightglass Group

TAKE YOUR TURN:
HOW CAN YOU MAKE TODAY COUNT?

1. What does the statement "Live life to the fullest and die empty" mean to you as a person?

_____

_____

_____

_____

_____

_____

2. What are some things that have kept you from living your full life today?

_____

_____

_____

_____

_____

_____

3. What difference would it make in your life if you lived today as if it was your last?

• In your personal life

_____

_____

_____

• In your family/relational life

_____

_____

_____

• In your career life

_____

_____

_____

• In your business/professional life

_____

_____

_____

4. What action(s) are you willing to take today to start living life to the fullest?

_____

_____

_____

_____

_____

_____

_____

CHAPTER 7

THE POWER OF TODAY

*To every man there comes in his lifetime that special
moment when he is figuratively tapped on the shoulder
and offered a chance to do a very special thing, unique
to him and fitted to his talents. What a tragedy if that
moment finds him unprepared or unqualified for that
which would be his finest hour.*

Sir Winston Churchill (1874-1965)
British Statesman, Army Officer, and Writer

History is replete with people who, for better or for
worse, seized their day and rewrote history as we know it
today. They either made or marred their "finest hour," as
Sir Winston Churchill once described it. All of the defining
moments in human history were once ordinary moments
until someone did something unusual with their ordinary
moment. Every day is a routine day until something
exceptional is birthed. This is also true with your life
and with mine. Each day is pregnant with destiny and
loaded with purpose. The recognition of this reality is the
unleashing of the magic therein.

One way to understand how historical figures took
advantage of their day is to examine what they said or did
in the crosshairs of the moment. What did they say? How
did they say it? Why did they say it? How did it change the
way forward? There is untold potential in each day and

in every single moment we live. The potential waits to be unleashed. Several people in history understood this concept and rose to the challenge of the moment. The actions they took and the opportunities they seized defined their era. In the sections below, I highlight a few of them as examples of how we can seize the moment too.

FIVE WAYS TO UNLEASH THE POWER OF TODAY

1. **Recognize Your Finest Hour: Lesson from Winston Churchill**

Sir Winston Churchill was born on November 30, 1874, to an aristocratic British father and an American mother from a wealthy family. The "greatest living Englishman," as he affectionately became known, did not live an idle life. In 1895, Sir Churchill was commissioned as a second lieutenant in the British Army. He used his mother's influence to obtain a post in a war zone.[13] Sir Churchill served as a military officer in Cuba, India, and South Africa. He would continue to live a robust life as a distinguished statesman. He served as a member of parliament for decades before becoming the British prime minister.

Taking over the premiership in May of 1940, Churchill was committed to the survival of Britain as a nation. This was in the midst of World War II, the deadliest military conflict in history. It is estimated that between 75 and

---

13 Gilbert, Martin (1991) Churchill: *A Life London*, Heinemann

85 million people perished, totaling nearly 3 percent of the world's entire population of 2.3 billion people at the time.[14] To further add to the unspeakable atrocity, specific demographics of people were being targeted, including Jews, the Roma population, and people with disabilities. It was a dark time in world history.

As Sir Churchill addressed the House of Commons on June 18, 1940, he likely knew the gravity his words could hold. We can imagine the pressure he felt as he attempted to influence the world and positively shape the future for generations to come. It is possible he was feeling the weight of the responsibility of surviving the impending war and preserving the British Empire. He knew that his actions alone wouldn't be enough; he needed to inspire every single person involved in the horrific war—whether they were a soldier, an administrator, or a citizen—to make the best possible use of the power they held. In an often-quoted and monumental speech, he said

> *But if we fail, then the whole world, including the United States, including all that we have known and cared for, will sink into the abyss of a new dark age made more sinister, and perhaps more protracted, by the lights of perverted science. Let us, therefore, brace ourselves to our duties and so bear ourselves that if the British Empire and its Commonwealth last for a thousand years, men will still say, This was their finest hour.*[15]

14 International Programs. Historical Estimates of World Population. U.S. Census Bureau 03-06-2013 Accessed 01-12-2021.
15 Excerpted from Winston Churchill's Speech to the House of Commons of the United Kingdom, June 18, 1940.

There comes a time in our lives when we realize that history is upon us. There are times when we must let go of our immediate fears and needs in life. We must skip forward a thousand years ahead and look back to where we stand at the moment. We must ask ourselves, how will the decisions we make affect future generations to come? How will we influence the world for the next thousand years? When we grasp the power of our daily decisions today and review them in retrospect, we may discover one of our simple moments turned into our "finest hour."

It's important not to take today for granted. We must be able to answer the question: How can we make today the *finest hour* that future generations will look back on with pride? How can we tap into the defining moments of our lives and create such a historic moment?

Today, this hour or this very minute could be part of that hour.

2. Have Faith in the Righteousness of Your Cause: Lesson from Mahatma Gandhi

In chapter 6 (Put a Demand on Today), we discussed how Gandhi led the Salt March with seventy-nine of his trusted peers on March 12, 1930. The oppressive salt tax affected every single Indian, from the wealthy to the poor; however, as is usually the case, the tax was particularly unjust to those who lived life on the margins of society due to extreme poverty and lack of access to resources.

When Gandhi stood up alongside his fellow congress leaders in 1930 to crack down on the British salt tax through a nonviolent protest march, he knew very well that this might earn him years of imprisonment by the British authorities or even cost him his life. These fears did not deter Mahatma, as he was affectionately called. Mahatma is a term that translates to mean the "great soul." Gandhi was clear in his resolve that none of these threats—not prison nor even death—would stop him. On March 11, 1930, the night before the great march would begin, Gandhi began his remarkable speech with these words:

> In all probability, this will be my last speech to you. Even if the government allows me to march tomorrow morning, this will be my last speech on the sacred banks of the Sabarmati. Possibly these may be the last words of my life here.

> Mahatma Gandhi

If Gandhi's opening words were moving, the conclusion of his riveting message was even more so. Gandhi is world-renowned for his powerful methods of nonviolence and passive resistance. He planted words of peace, stirring inspiration in the hearts of those listening by reminding them that they, too, could continue with the work of protesting the government's oppressive actions. He went on to say:

> I believe there are men in India to complete the work begun by me. I have faith in the righteousness of our cause and the purity of our weapons. And where the means are clean, there God is undoubtedly present with His blessings.

How, in the face of great risks to his own life, did a human being take on such a great challenge? The answer rests in the words above, "I have faith in the righteousness of our cause and the purity of our weapons." The Great Soul refers to the weapons of peace and the strength of the unity of those who act upon the unwavering convictions of their righteous beliefs.

Can you think of the last time you had faith in the righteousness of your life's purpose or cause? When was the last time you believed in the purity of your weapons? Are you secure in the faith that love and positivity always prevail? Do you believe we are called upon to use our weapons of peace for our benefit and for those who come after us? Sadly, our everyday living often lacks a sense of purposefulness. This absence of a backbone does not allow us to seize the moment and experience the power of today. What could we do if we had Gandhi's courage and strength of conviction in our sense of purpose? Could we use a tool as simple as the cause for daily salt to change the world?

Find a righteous cause and invest your faith in it.

Choose the purity of means and bring it to life.

3. **Beware of the Perils of Indifference:**
    Lesson from Elie Wiesel (1928–2016)

Eliezer Wiesel was born in September 1928 in the mountainside town of Sighet, Romania, to traditional, devout Jewish parents. He experienced firsthand what life was like in the Nazi concentration camps in 1944 before being liberated by U.S. soldiers on April 11, 1945, when he was just sixteen years old. His mother and sister were not as fortunate. They were murdered at Auschwitz. His father perished from harsh slave labor and starvation before he had the chance to be liberated.

After surviving such horrific experiences, Wiesel became a journalist in Paris and a celebrated author of fifty-seven books written in English and French. One of the most notable was his memoir of the Holocaust, entitled *Night*. He further earned professorships at Yale, City University of New York, and Boston University. He was awarded the Nobel Peace Prize in 1986 for speaking out against violence, repression, and racism, and the United States Presidential Medal of Freedom in 1992, among many other distinguished awards and honors from around the world.

On April 12, 1999, at the brink of the new millennium, President Bill Clinton, First Lady Hillary Clinton, and members of Congress gathered to hear Elie Wiesel speak about the past, the present, and the future. The title of the speech was "The Perils of Indifference." Wiesel cautioned against the dangers of living life as if there is no difference when people are marginalized and unchecked power runs rampant. He warned that indifference could be tempting— even seductive! He even challenged, "Better an unjust God than an indifferent one." Wiesel recalled the "righteous rage" of the American soldiers who liberated him from

Buchenwald concentration camp. He noted that anger ignites action, whereas indifference leaves people to suffer, forgotten, full of despair, and with no possibility of hope. He shared several examples of hopeless, emaciated people covered in blankets, thinking the world had forgotten about them. He added that when we deny others' humanity, we deny our own.

One-time U.S. presidential candidate, former U.S. Secretary of State, and former Senator of New York Hillary Clinton described Wiesel as one who "taught us never to forget," further sharing that Wiesel "made sure that we always listen to the victims of indifference, hatred, and evil." Clinton quoted Wiesel as saying, "In the place where I come from, society was composed of the killers, the victims, and the bystanders." Wiesel warned that it's "so much easier" to look away from victims and avoid "rude interruptions" to our work, dreams, and hopes. He contended that indifference is always the friend of the enemy.

Wiesel's experience and lessons teach us about the perils of being indifferent to daily actions around us. Indifference, a friend of the enemy, can appear like a wolf in sheep's clothing. Its harm is tangible but unnoticed. Its dangers are unthinkable yet unseen.

If today must be lived in the power that it represents, it cannot, should not, and must not be indifferent. We must make a conscious choice not to be bystanders in our generation. We must decide to act when we should and how we should, regardless of how uncomfortable it is to us at the moment. Indifference means "no difference." If we act with indifference, the world will be no better because of our presence in it.

When was the last time you acted in a manner as to unlock indifference? When was the last time you embraced courage in your life?

Remember, recognizing indifference and having the courage to act on what you see is the power you hold today.

4. **Fear Only Fear Itself:**
   Lesson from Franklin Roosevelt (1882–1945)

Franklin Delano Roosevelt was the thirty-second president of the United States from 1933 until he died in 1945. During his presidency, he dealt with the Great Depression and World War II, the greatest crises of the time. He knew that apathy and indifference were not an option. He defeated President Herbert Hoover in a landslide election. The country was ready for hope, change, and leadership.

In the president's inaugural address on March 4, 1932, he famously stated, "The only thing we have to fear is fear itself." He courageously held powerful bankers accountable for the nation's economic destruction, pointing out how greed and apathy had decimated the country. He noted in his speech that "now was the time to speak the truth, the whole truth, frankly, and boldly." He further highlighted the painful truth that leaders who placed profit above all else, even humanity, were "stripped of the lure of profit," which seduced people to follow their false leadership. He confidently assured those weary from poverty and war that the great nation of the United States would once again "revive and prosper."

He noted that values had "shrunken to fantastic levels" and that unemployed citizens were facing the "grim problem of existence." He warned, "Only a foolish optimist could deny the dark realities of the moment."

Thanks to the weakened state of the economy, the United States was vulnerable to outside attacks. But through courage, determination, and commitment to fearlessness, President Roosevelt pulled his country through one of the most vulnerable periods of American history. Courage is powerful. President Roosevelt understood this. He did not let fear stop him.

How does fear impact your life and keep you from making decisions that could maximize the power of today? Who is impacted by your lack of inaction? Who could be helped, and how many generations could be served if you seized the power of today?

5. Hold Onto an Ideal Worth Dying For: Lesson from Nelson Mandela

Former South African president Nelson Mandela is referenced throughout this book—not without cause. He lived a profound life with unimaginable challenges. I believe that his example illustrates the very essence of this book: namely, that tomorrow can only count if we make today count.

In Mandela's autobiography, *The Long Walk to Freedom* (a 115-chapter-long treatise), we observe example after example of how he seized the power of each day despite the dire circumstances that surrounded his life.

President Mandela spent twenty-seven years of his adult life in prison and never in those years forgot his mission, focus, or why he was there. He even used his access to help other prisoners. As he was somewhat famous, admirers would send him food that was much nicer and more abundant than the food given in prison. He would only accept it if he could share it with the other prisoners.

When the prisoners were subjected to an abusive warder[16], Mandela would use his influence to get them a warder who would act with more humanity. He wielded so much power and was respected even in a prison cell. It was strange that a prisoner could carry that much influence.

---

16 Another term for prison warder is correctional services officer.

Under the light of the world, Mandela spoke out at his trial on April 20, 1964. He stated:

> *During my lifetime, I have dedicated myself to this struggle of the African people. I have fought against white domination, and I have fought against black domination. I have cherished the ideal of a democratic and free society in which all persons live together in harmony and with equal opportunities. It is an ideal which I hope to live for and to achieve. But if needs be, it is an ideal for which I am prepared to die.*

Sometimes we feel powerless in our lives. We think there's not much we can do to change the world. Reflecting on how Mandela literally laid his life down for his people instructs us on how we can live today. It teaches us that we ought not only to find something we would live for but, even more crucial, embrace a cause we would die for.

How can you seize the power of today to better the world? Is there a cause in your life so great that you are willing to die for it?

CONCLUSION

There is power in every mundane action we take if we do so with the full understanding that consequences will accrue, for better or worse. The bravest among us teach us that there are no extraordinary people nor extraordinary days—just ordinary people on ordinary days doing extraordinary acts.

You might recall the story of my dear friend Pastor Kevin Taylor, who experienced an unexpected heart attack during a workout class in chapter 1 ("The Illusion of Tomorrow"). You would remember that Phil, the gym manager, had made a routine decision to change the battery of the AED days before the incident, not knowing that it would save a life.

Think about the CPR-certified classmate, Avery, who administered CPR and actually used the AED and shocked my friend's heart back to life! I have learned that life-changing acts do not necessarily look heroic when the decisions are made. We only appreciate how heroic these were in hindsight. I am so thankful to Phil and Avery for the life of my dear friend. My church congregation will always be grateful for these ordinary citizens who acted in ways that turned a near-death experience into an unforgettable story of salvation.

In my own life, I have experienced an ordinary moment turning into a defining moment when viewed in hindsight. Early in January of 2021, I was in Cameroon, Central Africa, hosting a dinner for LEAD Missions International, one of the organizations I lead, when a team member, Jonah, shared a story. "Last year, I attended a team meeting of conference organizers and workers," he began.

He then looked in my direction and continued, "While you were addressing a room full of conference staffers,

I remember you challenging us to embrace our personal growth. After your speech, you walked up to me and said, 'I don't want to meet you on the same spot when I return next year.'"

Jonah shared how these words stuck in his memory in the twelve months that followed. He recalled saying to himself, "I must not be in this same spot by next year. I must do something that will change the course of events in my life."

I have known my friend Jonah for nearly twenty years. I have had the honor of using his services as a professional driver. Through the years, we have grown close, and so have our families. Jonah had listened to several of my speeches through the years, but he said that the words of this particular talk hit him in the heart.

Within twelve months, Jonah would secure a business license, start a real-estate venture, and begin construction on a three-level, eighteen-bedroom complex—all from nearly no savings a year ago. He told me how this project is symbolic of the power of believing in himself and his ability to achieve what he set out to do. He told me that he now believes nothing is impossible and that this experience was a defining moment in his life.

When Jonah told me this story of how my words empowered him to break through his own self-limiting beliefs, defy self-perceived inadequacies, and create possibility thinking, I was so humbled.

I did remember my words to him. But they didn't seem particularly forceful in themselves, or so I thought, to yield the results that they did. The full effect of these words seemed to go beyond his current outcomes. It was a mind-shift, a change of paradigm, which is still creating new results every day.

The story tells of how an ordinary driver, living on monthly wages of about $2,000, received faith to believe in a future that was a thousand times bigger and greater than what he could ever have imagined. It all began with an ordinary discussion, an ordinary friendly charge, to decide to do things differently and reject stagnation. I cannot tell you how proud I am of this friend of over twenty years.

Each ordinary day of our lives is loaded with extraordinary opportunities waiting to be unlocked. *The ability to recognize each of these "fine moments"—often packaged in vessels of ordinariness—will determine how far we go and how high we rise in life.* Don't forget it or miss the opportunity.

Take hold of your today!

TAKE YOUR TURN:
HOW CAN YOU MAKE TODAY COUNT?

1. What have been some of your "finest hour" moments in life?

_____

_____

_____

_____

_____

_____

_____

2. What are some fears that have kept you from maximizing these "finest hour" moments?

_____

_____

_____

_____

_____

_____

3. What difference would it make in your life if you embraced your "finest hour" moments:

• In your personal life

_____

_____

_____

• In your family/relational life

_____

_____

_____

• In your career life

_____

_____

_____

• In your business/professional life

_____

_____

_____

4. What action(s) are you willing to take today to deal with fear and live purposefully?

_____

_____

_____

_____

_____

_____

_____

CHAPTER 8

PURPOSE, BIG PICTURE, AND PLAN

*"Your big picture will never be a masterpiece
if you ignore the tiny brushstrokes."*

Andy Andrews
New York Times bestselling author
and critically acclaimed international speaker

I have always believed that the key to a satisfying life is intentional living. When we don't embrace intentional living, we default to accidental existence. Intentional living means that we understand our purpose in life, embrace the big picture of how to achieve that purpose, and have a plan to do so.

The purpose of any task or activity is in its *why*. It is its reason for being. We all start small and grow into fulfilling our *why* as we get along in life. While everyday living demands that we know how to manage the minutiae of our lives, it is difficult to be truly successful if we do not keep the big picture in mind. It's like the whole picture in a puzzle game. It guides our everyday pieces to be properly fitted together. However, to fit all the pieces together to form the big picture, we need some kind of plan. This chapter's focus is to provide some guidance as to how we can discover purpose, embrace our big picture, and plan our *today* more efficiently.

PURPOSE

Begin Small, But Believe Big

I learned a lot about purpose growing up with my grandfather in the grasslands of Cameroon in Central Africa. As I mentioned in chapter 4, my grandpa developed a nervous disorder due to an improperly administered injection around a nerve, leaving him partially paralyzed. He suffered from this condition for the remainder of his life.

When I was young, Grandpa would share his dreams and aspirations, even though he was now managing some challenging health issues. Although he could no longer practice as a nurse, he saw himself as a community transformer. That sense of purpose guided him in his nursing career, and it also guided him when he became a farmer.

I remember wondering, at six years old, "When does he think he will achieve all these things?" Although I was young, I knew he had mobility issues and wondered how he would accomplish his goals and dreams with his physical impairment. Grandpa continued living his life, pursuing his purpose of being a community change agent, despite his health challenges. In the thirty years that followed his career as a nurse, he sat on the village council, became a member of the customary court, wrote a book, advised hundreds of villagers, raised many children and grandchildren, and became a farmer.

Looking back at Grandpa Simon's life, I see him as a purposeful transformer. He taught our community that agriculture could go beyond mere subsistence. Reinventing farming practices was a novel and revolutionary idea at the time for many of the villagers. My grandpa taught me how to grow rice, coffee, mangoes, pineapples, avocado, plums, bananas, and guava, among many other fruit trees. An acreage of fruit trees surrounded our village home.

My grandpa also taught the villagers how to make money from cash crops. He educated the young on how to earn a decent living. He challenged laziness in the youth and encouraged hard work. He believed life was precious and recognized that every day was a gift. Since he didn't know how many days his condition would allow him to live, he committed himself to God, who knew all things. He often would call me to sing his favorite hymn along with him. The very first line of this hymn, to me, summarized his entire belief, "My hope is built on nothing less than Jesus' blood and righteousness."[17]

I remember sitting with him for hours as he dictated the book he was writing to me or asked me to read a typewritten copy of it. He told me, "I have a message for the president of the nation. When this book is finished, I would like him to have a copy and respond to the contents of it." As a little child, I wondered how Grandpa would get his book from our small village to our nation's

17 *On Christ the Solid Rock I Stand* (Hymn by Edward Mote, 1934)

capital. Grandpa was confident. He instructed my uncle, "Emmanuel, make sure this book reaches the president."

While I am not sure Grandpa's manuscript ever reached the president's desk, I know he sent a copy his way. The moral of this story is that I grew up around a family member who had a strong sense of purpose, regardless of the path his life led him on. Grandpa became an honorary father to an entire village—honored and respected by its people.

Several years later, as an adult, I found myself in America, thousands of miles away from home. Without much money to my name or knowing how I would accomplish my goals, a stroke of destiny brought back memories of my early childhood with Grandpa, who had since passed away. There were moments I could hear his voice in my head. I'd hear some of his favorite quotes, including, "Common sense is not common, Madison" or "Common sense is not taught in any school." He often used these sayings to help me understand the value of conventional wisdom.

I had arrived in the United States filled with dreams and aspirations, but my financial circumstances constantly threatened the picture of who I was and why I was here. At times I couldn't believe that my dreams were possible. However, then I remembered my grandpa's simple vision to transform our small village community through little acts of love and kindness. I remembered his tenacity, passion for serving the community, and willingness to work in any capacity that would help engrave his name in the hearts of thousands over his lifetime. Grandpa did all this with the devastating blow of losing his career as a nurse. He did not let his physical disability limit him. Based on his example, I knew I could do something with my own life.

Like Grandpa Simon, I knew I could begin small but keep believing big. Grandpa took small steps to reinvent his life, still holding onto his sense of purpose, and after a tragedy that seemingly altered his life for the worse, he ended up thinking, "The president could read my book." I believed the same could be true for me, too, regardless of the circumstances. Whether I participated in gutting a dilapidated home in post-Hurricane Katrina New Orleans for an appreciation fee, labored as a security officer, or distributed marketing ads on the streets of New Orleans East, there was always this deep sense of purpose. I had a feeling that spoke to me and said, "You can be somebody. You were born for a higher purpose."

When our sense of purpose drives us, the small brushstrokes in the painting of our life likely will not make sense to anyone else. It's not important that they do. When we are driven by our goal to fulfill the reason we are living this life, at this moment, our actions will make sense to us. A financial planner might have thought I was crazy to do the work I was doing with the seemingly insurmountable debt I was facing. However, I knew the small steps I was taking would help me fulfill my big-picture plan.

As I embraced this inner conversation and accepted it to be true, I found myself calling a few immigrant friends to share this wisdom. I assembled my friends on a conference call to share encouragement and challenge them to believe in their dreams so they, too, would find the courage to stay on their path of a greater purpose. We called it the Mentoring Forum back then. The Mentoring Forum became the precursor of conferences and seminars we now run today through my organization, LEAD Missions International. The group has grown from a few of my immigrant friends to conferences featuring participants from tens of countries worldwide, including presidents, senators, congressmen, professionals, clergy, and others interested in progressing in their purpose. The humble Mentoring Forum is now known as the MenLEAD and Leading Lady conferences and seminars.

Purpose is powerful!

Author Jim Kwik highlighted a conversation he had with actor Jim Carrey in his recent book, *Limitless: Upgrade Your Brain, Learn Anything Faster, and Unlock Your Exceptional Life.* Carrey shared:

> *The purpose of my life has always been to free people from concern... How will you serve the world? What do they need that your talent will provide? That's all you have to figure out... The effect you have on others is the most valuable*

currency there is. Everything you gain in life will rot and fall apart, and all that will be left of you is what you have in your heart.

However simple your purpose may seem, if it uses your gifts and helps others, it will undoubtedly be very powerful and transform the lives of many.

WHAT IS PURPOSE, AND HOW DO WE FIND IT?

As I've stated before, purpose speaks to the *why* of an activity or a goal. I believe that just as every product has an inherent purpose intended by its manufacturer, every human is a carrier of their purpose. Hence, we discover our purpose as we go through life; we *do not* create one for ourselves.

Renowned leadership expert John C. Maxwell shares some pointers in his book, *Developing the Leader Within You 2.0*, regarding developing and owning our vision. I find his wisdom so applicable in the discovery of purpose. We can discover purpose by observing ourselves in these five key areas I adapted from Maxwell's framework.

1. **Look within you:**
    Ask, "Who am I?" and "Why am I here?"

Questions such as "Who am I?" or "Why am I here?" are questions of purpose. They speak to what you are to represent based on your unique calling. These questions call on us to take a deep introspective look at life to answer even deeper questions: "What are my gifts? What are my talents? What is natural to me? What am I drawn to? What makes me cry? What makes me happy?" Each one of these questions is an indicator of one's true purpose in life.

The things that make us angry point us toward what we do not want. They direct us to what we were probably born to change or eradicate. What makes us laugh is a guide to a desire and peace we want to keep. The positive feelings we have indicate the environment we want to preserve and perpetuate.

2. **Look behind you:**
   "What does my life story reveal to me?"

Everyone has a past. Unfortunately, people frequently use their past against themselves. They may even use their memories and experiences to hurt themselves. The past is meant to guide us to the life we were uniquely fashioned to live. There is no mistake as to where you were born, the circumstances surrounding your upbringing, and the experiences you have lived. Each of these situations made you who you are today and gave you an uncommon edge, insight, and drive that no one else on the surface of the earth possesses.

However, it takes work to understand that our life's history is a gift before we can take advantage of the lessons we've learned. I remember my upbringing, growing up in a small African village with no running water and no power supply. I recall how children my age back then sometimes did not have basic necessities like shoes to wear or food to eat every day. My experiences have made me see poverty as the enemy and become a crusader for our communities' financial freedom.

3. **Look around you: Ask,**
   "What do people closest to me see in me?"

Why do people like me? What is it about me that they admire? What draws them to me? These are all insights into what your purpose might be. The qualities they are drawn to in you identify a need met in them as they hang out around you. If we pay close attention to the genuine affirmations, compliments, and praise that others give us—unsolicited—we will get a clue of our "*why.*"

4. **Look above you: Ask,**
   "What does God expect of me?"

There's something bigger than ourselves out there that, if we seek it, will humble us as humans. We always have to look beyond ourselves for a cause bigger than ourselves; otherwise, our actions will seem empty. As we find a purpose bigger than ourselves, we will discover a *divine calling* to do that which only we can do. Our history, gifts, talents, and the people we interact with have all brought us to where we are meant to be. This sense of purpose, I believe, is always there whether we realize it or not. To access it, we only need to "look up"!

5. **Look ahead: Ask,**
   "What do I see in my future?"

Dreams and aspirations are the things that move us, the things that energize us, excite us, and make us want to live one more day. And yes, they provide our sense of hopefulness. All these are pointers to purpose. We only dream who we are on the inside. We can only see the picture of the future that is uniquely tied to our inner sense of purpose. Paying attention to your dreams and aspirations is a great way to stay focused. It's been my observation that successful people never lose this sense of hopefulness and dreaming, and because they do, they live their purpose.

BIG PICTURE

I shared in chapter 1 of this book that anyone can tell the number of seeds in an apple, but God alone can tell the number of apples in a seed. If the purpose is the seed, then harvest is the big picture. It is the picture of the harvest in the farmer's mind that inspires him to sow a seed. He sows in toil and labor; he reaps in joy and satisfaction. It is in anticipation of the harvest that the farmer sows his seed. In much the same way, it takes seeing the big picture of our "harvest" to live a life of purpose.

Living life with a big-picture perspective is very important. Big-picture living allows you to take the hopefulness of tomorrow to inspire today. Let me ask you a question: How would you act today if you knew that your dream of tomorrow was completely possible and that there were no chances for failure? Most likely, you'd act confidently and totally motivated. And this is ultimately why the big picture is essential. It gives meaning to today's drudgery and its mundane tasks.

Tomorrow is an inspiration, yesterday is a lesson, and today is the crossroad of inspiration and relevant experience that can change our lives. What seed are you? If you don't know what seed you are, you can't possibly tell what orchard you are becoming. Olive seeds only produce olive orchards, and orange seeds only create orange orchards. Our orchard of destiny is hidden in the seed of our today. We must be able to tap into who we *are* and *why* we are. Big-picture living helps us achieve this.

One benefit of big-picture living is that we cease to compare ourselves with others. For what comparison has oranges with apples? Aren't they unique creations? In much the same way, every human being bears a unique seed inside of them. The recognition of who we truly are singles us out from the maze of all human beings—past, present, and future. However, without a big picture, our lives would be fraught with confusion, frustration, and apathy. We will feel helpless.

THE PLAN

The plan is the strategy we use for converting the *seed* inside us into the *harvest* of our lives. Every dream without an actionable plan is a nightmare in disguise. It takes several action steps to get to the result. It has been aptly said that people do not plan to fail; they only fail to plan. A well-thought-out plan is what separates *wishers* from *achievers*.

Let me ask you a personal question: do you have a plan for your life, family, career, finances, or business? We seize the day when we develop a plan and commit our lives to its achievement.

This way of life is neither easy nor perfect. As Nelson Mandela said, "It always seems impossible until it's done." Committing to a plan is never a perfect science; nonetheless, it yields the joys we desire if we offer ourselves to it.

LET'S SUM IT UP!

Start each day with purpose. The purpose and big-picture plan will purify your motives and offer guidance by focusing you on the priorities that will help fulfill your purpose. However, you must keep the big picture in mind. Some daily worries and occupations will not make sense when evaluated in light of the big picture. When examined in the light of the big picture, being distressed about the past, something that is gone forever, makes no sense at all. Once we understand our purpose, the next step is to have a plan.

Even an imperfect plan is better than no plan. Remember, too, that plans are amendable and do change. As Mike Tyson, former world heavyweight champion and the "greatest of all time" boxer, once said, "Everybody has a plan until they get punched in the mouth." Our plans might suffer a reset, necessitating a return to purpose, big picture, and back to a new plan.

Do you have a purpose? Do you see your big picture? And do you have a plan?

TAKE YOUR TURN:
HOW CAN YOU MAKE TODAY COUNT?

1. What would you say has been your *purpose* in life?

_____

_____

_____

_____

_____

_____

_____

2. What would you say is the *big picture* that you need to keep you on your life's path?

_____

_____

_____

_____

_____

_____

_____

3. What difference would it make in your life if you embraced your *purpose*, *big picture*, and *a plan...*

• In your personal life

_____

_____

_____

• In your family/relational life

_____

_____

_____

• In your career life

_____

_____

_____

• In your business/professional life

_____

_____

_____

4.   What plan(s) are you willing to make today to move you towards a better future?

_____

_____

_____

_____

_____

_____

_____

CHAPTER 9

THE BEST DAY EVER!

*"Your best day ever is a today that is lived through
the inspiration of the possibilities of tomorrow
and the lessons of yesterday."*

Madison Ngafeeson

Your best day ever is not when you wake up and
discover that all your challenges are gone. It's not the day
you rise to greet a perfect world. It's not even the day you
scale your highest mountain. I'll dare say that your best day
is not even an event! It is not a destination.

Your best day ever is a state of being. It is an attitude
and a resolve that says, "I will live today with the
hopefulness of tomorrow and the mindfulness of the
lessons of yesterday. I am committed to the right actions I
must take today."

Once you are aware of the power of today, you'll begin
to see opportunities all around you, even in the most
unlikely circumstances. No matter what is going on in the
world, there is always hope. There are always possibilities.
There are always solutions. While this concept might seem
easy to believe in theory, it's life-changing to experience
embracing the possibilities of today yourself and to witness
others doing the same.

I started to write *The Day Before Tomorrow* early in 2020. The dream was planted in my heart years before when I attended a John Maxwell conference. He encouraged the attendees by challenging us with the thought that *our story was the greatest story ever told.* This reality seemed to have taken a deep root in me.

I wholeheartedly believe in the power of today, and the COVID-19 pandemic gave me countless opportunities to deepen this belief. I experienced the breadth of possibility in my own life as I saw the Lead Missions International conferences (the nonprofit I founded) go from in-person attendance of some hundreds of people to now reaching thousands of people in fifty-five countries around the world through the use of online platforms. It taught me *possibility thinking!*

POSSIBILITY THINKING

On the subject of possibility thinking: in 2020, I experienced firsthand how embracing what is seemingly impossible allows us to achieve heights we are unable to imagine. I learned this from a couple who lead a church organization in Mission, Texas, on whose board I currently serve. Freedom Life Church is located in a town of just over eighty-three thousand people. I've been involved since the church's inception in 2010, have acted as a leader, and ultimately became a board member in 2017.

When the church was established, the desire had always been to operate fully debt-free, not only for the church as an organization but for any individual who passes through its doors. This dream and desire were revisited often, and Pastors Eliud and Cathy Garcia believed this would be made possible one day.

Pastor Eliud Garcia of Freedom Life Church shared that he felt a stirring in his heart in October 2019. He passionately shared with anyone who would listen, "God wants us to be debt-free! Now is the time!" He thought becoming debt-free was the perfect way to celebrate the church's tenth-anniversary milestone.

The seed was planted; *now* was the time. Although the idea had been agreed to long ago, Pastor Garcia still needed official board approval to proceed. The board agreed that the idea was a good one; however, they were a little cautious. They did not understand exactly how the church would achieve such a significant undertaking. I was a little reluctant, too; however, I listened and participated in the conversations, knowing that all things are possible with God. The board worried that some members might stop giving altogether if they felt pressure to give even more.

Although the board's response was not quite what he would have wanted, Pastor Garcia did not let this deter him. He acknowledged that the board was doing their job, as it was their role to protect the church. Even still, Pastor Garcia felt confident that he should move forward, although he had never accomplished anything of this magnitude before. He was sure the goal was possible for the members, anyone who ever attended a service, and the church.

Pastor Garcia assembled a volunteer team and created a committee. He knew there would be strong Christians on the team, but he also needed sound businesspeople. The committee consisted of skilled church staff members and volunteers. He was aware that there would be disagreements, tension at times, and pushback on ideas. He was equally open to whatever would occur because he did not know how this was going to transpire. He was aware that they would need to be open to opinions and guidance from all committee members. With an assembly of such strong, talented, and opinionated people, he knew it would not be an easy path.

Although he was confident in the wisdom of his committee, he still felt he needed more counsel. He called other pastors he knew who had accomplished the goal of being debt-free. Some people shared that there were professional companies available to help and that they would normally charge twenty to thirty percent of the total funds they raised. Pastor Garcia listened to the advice; however, it didn't feel right to him to add more expenses when they were attempting to eliminate debt. He decided not to follow this advice.

He felt a little pressure from ignoring the guidance of the pastors, sage people who had already achieved the goal of being debt-free. He felt God was saying, "This is not Freedom Life Church's journey. This is not how you all are supposed to proceed." Again, Pastor Garcia listened to the message in his heart and cautiously moved forward, despite his subtle misgivings.

The newly-formed committee began to brainstorm ideas on how they would raise funds to manifest this idea. To become debt-free, the church would have to pay off the mortgage on their 12.83-acre property and the three buildings that occupied it. One building housed the main sanctuary, the nursery, the café, and the church offices. The second building contained the youth church and elementary and middle-grade worship rooms. The third building was primarily rented by a nearby nonaffiliated church that provided Spanish-language services. Thus, in addition to mortgages, there was a multitude of expenses necessary to fulfill their purposes.

Ideas were being batted around, including naming a building after someone or a corporation that could then give a large donation. Pastor Eliud pondered it and decided that wouldn't be right. He strongly believed that anyone who gave $500 was just as important as someone who gave $5,000. He relayed that the percentage of what someone had to give was more important than the dollar amount. He also felt strongly that the offering should not be coerced or rewarded in any way. He decided that any gifts received would not be made for any type of exchange.

Freedom 2020

By January 2020, Pastor Garcia and his church were ready to launch! The energy and encouragement were palpable. The church leadership prepared to make the big announcement of the church's plan to become debt-free, which would be called Freedom 2020! The committee cautioned that the goal should not be about the dollar amount or each person's actions. The messaging was important. Freedom 2020 was more about pulling people together than a dollar amount or a specific fundraising tactic. The essential communication was that the church would become debt-free, and each church member and anyone who believed in Freedom Life Church's vision *would also be debt-free.* Pastor Garcia stated, "We assured them it was all about building this together. It was about listening to and trusting what God wants us to do in our lives. It was also about supporting each other and strengthening our community."

The church planned a big celebration to launch Freedom 2020. Those who gave and those who didn't were all welcome to attend. He felt it was important that each individual was welcomed and included in the celebration, regardless of their means or ability to contribute. I was impressed that he was so inclusive! He loved all regardless of their actions or situations. Pastor Garcia commented, "That is *truly* living the mission of Freedom Life Church and the fearless path God wants us to follow."

Freedom Life Church was and is open to all. However, people commit to the church at different levels depending on their interests and ability to contribute. Members consist of people who commit to the mission and vision of the church and attend services. Members also make a financial commitment, often tithing 10 percent of their income. The congregation includes anyone who attends Freedom Life Church. Members and congregants were excited and engaged in the vision. They all discussed how they would make contributions since they considered Freedom Life Church to be their home church, whether they were formal members or not.

Those that were tithing were thinking of ways they could give more. Everyone was inspired that they were included in the vision. Not only would the church become debt-free, *but they, too, would become debt-free.* They started to envision what life would be like without a mortgage, personal loans, or credit card debt. No one was sure how it could be done; however, they were confident that it was possible and that God would reveal the path if their faith stayed strong and they remained committed to the goal.

The vision of becoming debt-free inspired a member

who did not even live in the area to donate $65,000 before the campaign was officially launched. This donor only attended the church via the web broadcast. However, Sally Johnson (actual name withheld for anonymity) was so moved by the church's mission of becoming debt-free that she wanted to contribute right away. She saw the church's mission as a cause worth sowing into. Pastor Garcia and the team could hardly believe the manifestation of such a generous donation from someone who did not live in the vicinity and was not available to attend services in person, even before the pandemic. The donation further inspired them to believe that God did want the church, the members, and the congregation to become debt-free and were confident they were on their way!

February 2020

In February 2020, the news of the deadly coronavirus hit the United States. By mid-March, the World Health Organization declared COVID-19 a global pandemic. The world began to shut down as state after state began to feel the impact of dealing with the extreme health risk. In April, May, and June, many people in the United States were either infected or affected by the consequences of the spread of the disease. Job losses, layoffs, and furloughs ensued as the nation struggled to find its financial balance.

Freedom Life Church's members and congregation were no different from the rest of America. They, too, were hit with the same struggles of shutdowns, social distancing, the uncertainty of the economy, the stresses of childcare, eldercare, and adjusting to homeschooling. Freedom 2020 was being battle-tested in real-time.

The enthusiasm for Freedom 2020 waned as people were beginning to feel hopeless and overwhelmed. The congregants questioned the wisdom of continuing with the goal under such dire circumstances. I must admit I wondered how this dream could ever come to life. I was questioning, too, whether pursuing Freedom 2020 was still a good idea. We were all experiencing a situation we had never even considered possible.

The big question was, "How can we ask people to give when they have just lost their job? How can we inspire hope when people's situations seem so desperate? How can we embrace faith when the fears are real and deep? How can we expect people to believe in the possibility of tomorrow when they can't see living past today?" The daily news coverage validated the grim future that seemed to lay ahead of everyone involved with Freedom Life Church.

Pastor Garcia was concerned, too; however, he remained steadfast in his belief. He reminded us that we'd had this goal for a long time, but he strongly believed that *now was the time*. He assured us when God speaks, we must move quickly. He admitted he was still committed to the goal. I thought he had a rather stubborn and unrelenting commitment to this goal. And though I, and maybe others, didn't understand how he could be so certain this was the right thing to do, Pastor Garcia assured all of us that he couldn't believe that God would touch his heart with such an idea and then not make it happen. He felt strongly; he was moved to do this *because of COVID-19* and all that was going on in people's lives. He was convinced that proceeding was the right thing to do, even when others thought he was, well—crazy.

Pastor Garcia shared that he took some time to answer the concerns. He prayed and ultimately concluded that God knew this pandemic was coming. God led them to achieve this goal now, and there must be a reason for it, even though the reason was not evident to anyone at the time. This realization gave him a sense of peace. He knew that others might not feel as certain as he did, which was okay.

All would be welcome to participate in the goal regardless of their situation or misgivings. When Pastor Garcia spoke to people about Freedom 2020, he was careful to acknowledge that this was a painful time. He would tell people to trust in God and have faith. He would profess, "God will do this with or without us." Pastor Garcia vowed to include every person in every celebration because the goal was to achieve becoming debt-free together. He was confident that this vision was more than just a money thing. It was to help people have stronger faith and trust that all things are possible when we follow the path God has laid out for us.

To keep people encouraged, Pastor Garcia would have members and the congregation share stories every time they paid off a credit card or any other debt. The positive stories ignited inspiration, and people began to see what was possible even when they dealt with their struggles. The church created celebration moments for every success. They demonstrated through these actions that the goal was not about money; it was about trust and faith that all things are possible if we follow what God lays into our hearts.

Although many businesses struggled, some enterprises prospered! When they did, the church celebrated their success. The stories motivated those who made pledges and shared hope with those who did not. The joy was infectious, and the celebrations kept everyone forging ahead. The celebrations were essential for all, as much of the world crumbled around them. This outreach was unprecedented for Freedom Life Church. They had never done anything like this, much less during a global crisis.

"Freedom Life Church had been created in 2010 to love people, not to raise money. God called the church to reach people," Pastor Garcia said. In addition to working on their financial goal, they donated to schools, helped neighbors in need, and checked in on the elderly and those who were alone. The church gave away thousands of lunches.

Pastor Garcia would remind everyone that "God did not give us a date. He just directed us to become debt-free." Donations kept coming in, and we continued to work toward the goal as a community. The jubilation of each gift and participant, whether they gave or not, was shared during live-streamed services or on the church's Facebook page when they could not meet in person. Although there was no set date, Freedom Life Church *became debt-free* in March 2021—exactly one year after the onset of the global pandemic.

Everyone rejoiced. Pastor Garcia shared the joy; however, he also felt relief and a deep sense of responsibility. He was happy and inspired by the deep relationships that were formed by all that were involved. However, he wondered, "What's next?" He had a multitude of emotions; they were not bad, but there was a lot to reflect on after the goal was achieved. He felt pressure to remain positive for others. However, he knew this was not the end. God had more in store for him, the church, and the world.

Pastor Garcia concluded that the seed God ignited in his heart and planted at Freedom Life Church in 2010 created a stronger faith and trust in all who participated. God's greatest gifts to the church were the sense of community, trust, collaboration, and focus on limitless possibilities; being debt-free was incidental.

LOOKING BACK AT THE
FREEDOM 2020 JOURNEY

I sat down with Pastor Garcia to understand all the lessons he had learned from achieving Freedom 2020 in just one year. Pastor Garcia eagerly shared the wealth of insights that were gained. These timeless lessons can help us all learn to maximize the power that exists in each new day.

Love and Trust

Trust one another and celebrate each other regardless of people's behaviors or circumstances in life. Pastor Garcia recalled that the lessons included trusting one another and celebrating one another regardless of our behaviors or circumstances in life. Some people did leave the church. Dealing with the pandemic and their own life challenges was just too much. People were sick; they lost their jobs; we can point to the graves of those who lost their lives. Yet the church released them with love. The lesson is not to love people only when they meet our expectations. We must love them regardless of life's circumstances and their actions.

Celebrate Each Day

Stay emotionally healthy. Celebrate every moment of every day. The church was careful to include all, especially those who could not give, so they wouldn't feel guilty. They were assured they were welcome and remained good friends. Their outside circumstances did not matter.

Don't Doubt in the Dark
What You Heard in the Light

Pay close attention to the feelings in your heart; the feelings have been placed in your heart to provide guidance. Undoubtedly, however, there will be obstacles, but you eventually see why these challenges were important. As Soren Kierkegaard, the Danish theologian, aptly commented, "Life can only be understood backward, but it must be lived forwards."

Tension Is Important

The tension between where we want to go and where we are is healthy. Even though we may be frustrated we are not where we want to be, we have advanced from where we used to be. The intersection of the discourse is today. Today is the transition point from what we used to be to the possibility of *where we could be*. Today is the launchpad for who we want to be from who we used to be.

We can channel all the lessons we have learned from the past to enable us to live our best day—today. Our hardships and successes, troubles and triumphs, trials and testimonials, sorrows and joys, and barriers and breakthroughs from the past are an essential part of living our best day yet. We cannot live in romantic memories of the past, no matter how positive. We cannot live in the optimism of a future that is not yet here. We can only embrace the gift of today, inspired by the hope of the possibilities of tomorrow and guided by the learnings of yesterday.

The Potential of the Seed
That Is Planted Today

Every human being has the ability to sense a stirring in their heart; it is a seed of the divine. Whether you think of this prompting as being from God or not, many people, regardless of their beliefs, resonate with a feeling stirring in their hearts. This idea, this seed, can be given the authorization to take root in our lives and create the harvest of a future that we truly desire.

The stories I have shared throughout this book demonstrate for you that listening to the messages that tug at your heart is *always* the right thing to do. The story in chapter 2 tells what my grandfather did when his professional nursing career was destroyed due to a disastrous medical error. In chapter 7, we discuss how Nelson Mandela influenced the greater good in the world while he was wrongly imprisoned for twenty-seven years. And in chapter 8, I relay what I did when I had no idea how I was going to pay my student loans, given every obstacle that appeared to be against me.

In each of these cases, trusting in the heart's convictions was pivotal. We must do today what will become the seed for tomorrow's possibilities. The power of today is immense. All we have to do is get out of our comfort zone and act in faith on our convictions. How lucky we are to learn how a little church in Texas, located in a community of fewer than a hundred thousand people, took the bull by the horns and did in the present what was near unbelievable. The voice is there if we choose to listen. The choice is ours.

WHAT ABOUT YOU?

Dream possibilities. Think possibilities. Live your full potential. Remember, you have the chance to begin again and follow the unique path of your individual life. You have the opportunity to share your perspectives, experiences, and skills to create a greater good not only for yourself, your family, and your friends but all of humanity.

Today is the only day we've been given. If somehow you forget this truth, remember your next morning is not promised. On the other hand, if you are lucky to greet a new day, recognize the day is bursting with possibilities.

Today is your best day ever, yesterday is gone forever, and tomorrow is not guaranteed. You have the gift of this very today and this very moment. Do not waste any of this moment thinking, worrying, or ruminating about yesterday. Burn the bridges of your past regardless of how painful the past might be—whether you did something you are not proud of, or something was done to you. It's over. This is today.

For some reason, we seem to gravitate toward

worrisome thoughts and visualizing negative outcomes. Yet no more effort is required to accept abundance, prosperity, and opportunity than is required to accept poverty and despair. Why are you making that choice? If something needs to be healed in you, make a resolution to learn how to heal it.

Conversely, spend your time thinking, "What brought me joy today? Have I expressed gratitude?"

Both despair and opportunity are born in thought. We can choose our thoughts and actions. Are your thoughts and actions aligned with your vision for your future? Which thoughts will you choose today? Those that propel you, or those that keep you stuck in the past?

Constantly challenge your perception barriers so that a world crisis or personal catastrophe will not have to push you to change and grow. We have the power to grow every day. Having faith in yourself and others, regardless of surrounding circumstances, will help push you to act today.

FIVE PERSPECTIVES TO MAKE TODAY YOUR BEST DAY EVER

1. **Understand That Your Inner Environment Is Always More Important than Your Outward Surrounding— Pay Attention to What Goes on Inside You!**

    Someone once said it is not the water that surrounds the ship that sinks her. It is the water that gets into her that does.

    We can act as thermometers, recording what is happening around us, or we can be thermostats, setting the temperature we desire to see in our world.

    The inner environment is the place of faith. It is that undying belief that this thing you are engaged in is worth its weight.

2. **Connect with Those Who Believe in Possibility without Totally Ignoring the Naysayers**

    People who do not think you will succeed have a reason why. Use their feedback wisely.

    Leadership guru John Maxwell says there are four kinds of people when it comes to relationships:

    1) Some people add something to life (we enjoy them).
    2) Some people subtract something from life (we tolerate them).
    3) Some people multiply something in life (we value them).
    4) Some people divide something in life (we avoid them).

3. **Revisit Your Dream to Draw Strength And, If Need Be, Revise Your Strategy**

Celebrate! Celebrate every minute of every day, every obstacle, and every success. Make changes and celebrate every progress. Celebrate the gift of today.

4. **Determine to Live a Life of No Regrets**

Ask yourself, "If I died today, would I regret not living my heart's dream?" Then, make sure the answer is a no!

5. **Understand That Who You Become Today Is More Important than What You Did Yesterday**

Remember that the greatest story ever told is the story of the person you became, given a hand you were dealt.

TAKE YOUR TURN:
HOW CAN YOU MAKE TODAY COUNT?

1. What *possibilities* do you see in your future?

_____

_____

_____

_____

_____

_____

_____

2. Which *major lessons* of yesterday have you learned that can improve on today?

_____

_____

_____

_____

_____

_____

_____

3. What will incorporating *possibilities* of tomorrow and the *lessons* of yesterday mean for you practically:

• In your personal life

_____

_____

_____

• In your family/relational life

_____

_____

_____

• In your career life

_____

_____

_____

• In your business/professional life

_____

_____

_____

4. Which of the *Five Perspectives of the Best Day Ever* would you want to start implementing, and how would you do that today?

_____

_____

_____

_____

_____

_____

_____

CHAPTER 10

THE DAY AFTER TOMORROW

"It doesn't matter to me any longer how long I live; what matters to me most is how I live!"

Trina Rigsby (1995-1996)
Loving first wife of Dr. Travis Rigby
mother of two devoted daughters.
A woman who lived fully
every day for forty-one years.

I have shared the stories of men and women who seized their day and accomplished tremendous feats throughout this book. Armed with the lessons of yesterday and the hopes of tomorrow, they did what they could with *their day* to change the world in significant ways. There is no denying that they created an impact in their world. However, the reason you seize the day and make *today* count is not only because of today. It's also because of tomorrow, and yes, the day after tomorrow.

In the introductory chapters of this book, I discussed that, while we have 365 days in each year, we essentially live in three days: yesterday, today, and tomorrow. In this chapter, I introduce the fourth day! I call it *the day after tomorrow*. The following breaks this concept down:

FOUR IMPORTANT DAYS

Yesterday

In chapter 1, I set the stage by discussing *the illusion of tomorrow*. Tomorrow is like the wind. No one has ever seen it, although we see evidence of the wind every time we watch the trees bow. Based on this evidence, we accept that wind exists. Even though we live in today and cannot see tomorrow, we often carry the worries of today into our tomorrow.

Yesterday, on the contrary, is a familiar topic for many. It's our longest day ever! We know it too well. Some of us talk about it all the time as if we were living yesterday today. There are no unknowns or possibilities in the topic of yesterday. We might be so familiar with yesterday that we make the unfortunate decision to use the precious gift of today to relive yesterday. Chapter 2 cautions on the dangers of driving forward while looking backward.

Today

Chapters 3, 6, and 7 were dedicated to the most important day of our lives—*today*! If we are lucky enough to wake up in the morning, today is a day to be seized. If we grasp the potential of today, we have the power to change our world. Today is also a day filled with resources. We have access to the lessons from failures and successes we experienced in our yesterday. We have the opportunity to learn from them and use those lessons to enhance our today. Today is full of potential. You can redefine yourself if you so choose.

Tomorrow

Then we discussed *tomorrow*. When I refer to *tomorrow*, I mean the future you have yet to live if you are fortunate enough to live in it. Tomorrow embodies your dreams, hopes, and aspirations! You might imagine that tomorrow is the day that will be created by the lessons of yesterday and the labor of today. When we live our today fully, learning from the lessons of yesterday, tomorrow becomes a "payday" of sorts.

The Day After Tomorrow

The day after tomorrow refers to the day when you are no longer here. All that will remain is the memory of the impact, or lack thereof, that you left. I believe that if we are to live today more amply and not just tap into both yesterday's lessons and tomorrow's hopes, we must live with the end in mind.

LIVE WITH THE END IN MIND

I believe that living life with the end in mind is crucial. When you accept this principle to be true, you will have three powerful incentives to make today count.

First, you will have the incentive to live more abundantly today, building upon the lessons of yesterday. Second, you will be motivated by the dreams and hopes you have for tomorrow—these dreams and hopes will cause you to engage your today more intentionally. And finally, you have the motivation of who you want to be remembered for beyond tomorrow when you are long gone. So let yesterday serve as your instruction; tomorrow, your inspiration; and the day after tomorrow, your motivation.

The great psychoanalyst Carl Jung commented, "As far as we can discern, the sole purpose of human existence is to kindle a light in the darkness of mere being." Unfortunately, many live their lives without thinking about the light that they are called to be. The day after tomorrow is about intentionally kindling a light and deliberately leaving a legacy. It's about what you leave behind for humanity.

Evangelist Billy Graham was one of America's most influential figures in recent history. He put it this way, "The greatest legacy one can pass on to one's children and grandchildren is not money or other material things accumulated in one's life, but rather a legacy of character and faith."

Tablets of Stone
Versus Tablets of Heart

There is a public cemetery about five miles from my home. I drive by it now and then. Sometimes when I have time, I'll stop the car and walk through this peaceful place. Some of the most fascinating things to catch my attention are the messages on the tombstones. I like to read what follows the words, "Here lies a (wo)man who...." I have often wondered how much of what is written on these tablets of stones is also inscribed on the tablets of the people's hearts who remember them.

I want my legacy to be in the hearts of humanity— tablets of men's and women's hearts—not just words on stones. A wonderful lady from South Texas, whom we're calling Sally Johnson, left a beautiful legacy and wrote on the hearts of her family and community profoundly.

Treasure in Vessels of Clay

You may recall that in chapter 9, I mentioned Mrs. Sally Johnson. She gave a significant donation of $65,000 to support the Freedom 2020 project, which led to a debt-free congregation. As I talked with the champions of this project, Pastors Eliud and Cathy Garcia, a married couple, they confessed, "This donation fueled our faith in the middle of a global pandemic to believe that our organization could be debt-free." Today, in part due to Sally's generosity, this organization is completely debt-free! Although Sally was only a "virtual member" of the church (attending service via live broadcast from out of town), she heard about the goal and wanted to be part of the mission.

What I did not tell you in chapter 9, however, is that Sally, a very successful businesswoman, passed away just eight months after making her donation. She had been diagnosed with a rare type of blood cancer four years prior, which the doctors said had no known cure.

At the time of her diagnosis, the doctor said, "Sally, I'm sorry, but you have a rare kind of leukemia that does not have a cure yet. We can certainly take advantage of chemotherapy, but it wouldn't cure you. I'm sorry."

The doctor reported that the typical life span after diagnosis was two years. At the time of her passing, Sally was seventy-three and had lived for *five years* after the diagnosis.

No one knows if we will live tomorrow, and no one can predict how many days we have on the earth.

Sally listened to this news and then built a plan for the remaining days she had in her life. She decided to live every day to its fullest, as healthy and clear-minded as possible. She refused all the chemotherapy treatments. Sally died surrounded by her loving husband of fifty-one years, her two sons, and several friends who loved her.

Pastor Cathy Garcia and Sally had been good friends for twenty-six years. When Cathy witnessed how Sally chose to live her last days, she was not surprised at all. Cathy shared, "She was a woman of faith, a giver, and a woman full of a sense of adventure. The day following her diagnosis, she had called me and said, 'Friend, let's go kayaking!'" And off they went! Living life to the fullest. Cathy further remembered, "She taught my children how to ski, and we had also gone on fishing trips together."

As I learned of Sally's story, I could not help but imagine her impact on all those who knew her. Family and friends at the burial testified of her love for people, her strength, faith, and her passion for adventure. Beyond all these who came to the funeral, I imagined the cause of becoming debt-free to which Sally seeded her $65,000. The organization's mission is couched in this belief: "We are servant leaders impacting our families, workplace, and the world with the love and power of a big God." Sally helped to manifest that mission with the actions she took in her life.

Freedom Life Church hosted an international leadership conference shortly after this in which people from thirty nations participated. I couldn't help but think that her legacy is engraved in the heart of every life that was impacted and every person that this organization will ever reach in the future.

Let your legacy take a permanent place in the hearts

of men and women. Make it your mission to write on tablets of the heart of humanity. This is what I mean when I say you must live with the end in mind. Beyond the here and now, what will your legacy be? Beyond a tombstone inscription, what will your message to the living be?

LET ME PAY THE PRICE FOR GREATNESS

As I speak at conferences and gatherings worldwide, I meet men and women who genuinely believe in, and want to live, a life bigger than themselves. They want to make a difference in their world and leave a legacy. But I have also noticed, sadly, that not everyone will achieve this level of greatness and leave a legacy that lives beyond the grave.

Not every dead person will speak to the living from beyond their grave. Not everyone leaves behind a legacy that lives on. However, the few that do, do it so significantly. I think you would agree with me that the world is ruled by dead men and women! By dead men and women, I mean the ideas of men and women who are no longer here but continue to influence humanity.

For instance, democracy is an idea. Communism is an idea. Capitalism is an idea. Those who conceived these ideas are in their graves today. Nonetheless, every day around the world, people are willing to stake their own very lives on these principles.

We will never live a life of greatness and significance without paying the full price upfront. I learned this from the story of Nelson Mandela, as told by Dr. Myles Munroe[18]. In his speech, Dr. Munroe told a story about a private dinner he attended; there were eighteen guests in all. The Nobel Peace Prize winner, former president of South Africa, attorney, and anti-apartheid activist Nelson Mandela was the guest of honor. During dinner, Mr. Mandela shook hands with the guests. When it was his turn, Munroe shook hands with Mandela too.

Dr. Munroe shared, "His hands felt like a rock." He relayed that he was visibly shocked, although he tried hard to hide it.

Concerned, Mandela asked, "Young man, are you okay?"

"Yes!" Munroe replied.

"No, you are not okay," retorted Mandela.

At this point, Munroe was embarrassed at what had just happened. He was shocked at the feel of Mandela's hard palm and couldn't hide it. Then, without leaving it to guesswork, Mr. Mandela explained to him how he was jailed for his fight against the apartheid regime in South Africa. During his prison days, he served in hard labor for about eighteen years of his twenty-seven-year jail term, breaking rocks. This made his hands calloused and hard.

---

18 Building a Legacy for the Next Generation Speech by Dr. Myles Munroe: https://www.youtube.com/watch?v=mZJmV1GAzv4

"This is the price of freedom!" exclaimed Mandela.

Hearing these words, looking at a man who had suffered such great indignities, Munroe felt a chill deep inside his bones. He remembers saying to himself, "Let me pay the price for greatness!"

Whatever it costs. Whatever it takes. Let's pay the price for true greatness. This is what legacy is all about—a life lived beyond one's self. A life lived for others. A life that transcends one lifetime. This is what *the day after tomorrow* is all about.

You might remember that in chapter 6, I shared that Dr. Munroe met an untimely death in 2014 in a tragic plane crash. He heeded former president Mandela's advice and left a profound legacy. He wrote more than fifty books, conducted many leadership conferences, seminars, and workshops, and spoke at international gatherings, encouraging audiences around the world to invest in people rather than buildings and transient symbols of success.

His words, example, and insights continue to live on and are written on the tablets of the hearts of countless men and women, including me. Like Munroe, who met president Mandela when he was a "young man," I heard Dr. Munroe speak when I was a freshman in college. His messages helped shape the course of my life. I had hoped to meet Dr. Munroe one day and was even planning a trip to the Bahamas. Unfortunately, the timing wasn't quite right.

While I never got to meet him in person, his words and legacy live on in me. I eagerly share his story and examples of his well-lived life, helping his messages to live on.

Former president Mandela, to date, remains one of the world's most revered figures of all times for his fight for human rights and justice. At his passing, to honor his life and legacy, South Africa had one of the world's largest gatherings of dignitaries, including two United Nations secretary generals, both presidents of the European Union (Council and Commission), two French presidents, four United States presidents, and four UK prime ministers. It is said that a total of more than five hundred VIP dignitaries from nineteen supranational organizations and nearly two hundred countries arrived for this event[19]. They came to pay homage to someone who left a legacy. They gathered to show respect to someone who had paid the price for greatness.

After he had heard the words of Mr. Mandela at the dinner, Dr. Munroe said, "I will never forget that moment." And he added, "I walked away from that table with a prayer, 'Oh Lord, make my hands hard. Let me pay a price for greatness!'"

I can't imagine a better prayer for myself. I can't imagine a better prayer for you. I can't imagine a better prayer for anyone who wants to make today count!

---

19 List of dignitaries at the memorial service of Nelson Mandela: *"Confirmation of foreign Heads of State and Government attending the memorial services or funeral"*. *South Africa Government Online. 9 December 2013. Archived from the original on 10 December 2013. Retrieved 9 December 2013*

"Let me pay a price for greatness!"

This is what legacy is all about—a life lived beyond one's self. A life lived for others. A life that transcends one lifetime. This is what *the day after tomorrow* is all about.

In conclusion, you were born to leave your contribution to humanity. You were born to make your mark—to leave your footprints on the sands of time! To do anything less is unacceptable. So pay the price. Make today count!

TAKE YOUR TURN:
HOW CAN YOU MAKE TODAY COUNT?

1. What would life mean for you if you lived with the end in mind?

_____

_____

_____

_____

_____

_____

_____

2. What legacy would you like to leave behind?

_____

_____

_____

_____

_____

_____

_____

3. What difference would it make *today* if you lived mindfully of *the day after tomorrow:*

• In your personal life

_____

_____

_____

• In your family/relational life

_____

_____

_____

• In your career life

_____

_____

_____

• In your business/professional life

_____

_____

_____

4. What action(s) are you willing to take today to live more intentionally?

_____

_____

_____

_____

_____

_____

EPILOGUE

It's been several years since I bought the book *The Greatest Story Ever Told*. It is the book I told you about in the Preface and that I have mentioned throughout this book. You might recall that this is the book that was filled with blank pages and how frustrated I was as I stared at the blank pages. I was so eager to learn about *The Greatest Story Ever Told*—and then disappointed to find 248 blank pages staring back at me.

Leadership expert John Maxwell's one-page note inscribed on the first page of the book began with these few, but profound words, "The Greatest Story Ever Told *can only be written by you!*" In some sense, and by writing this book, I attempted to fill some of these empty pages with my story.

It's now "248 pages" later; nonetheless, the central message of the book still holds true, "The Greatest Story Ever Told *can only be written by you! The greatest story ever told is not this one I have written. It is the one *you* will write! It is the one still to be written, the one that can only be written by *you*! If you choose not to write it, then, sadly, your unique story will be buried in the cemetery, in the company of those that did not share their unique contributions.

Many years ago, I read the story of the Queen of Sheba from ancient Ethiopia. She had heard of the wisdom of King Solomon of the distinguished Kingdom of Israel. So right around 1000 BC, she and her servants journeyed more than two thousand miles to experience Solomon's fame and wisdom they had heard so much about. She was curious and wanted to witness this greatness herself.

After spending approximately six months in the Kingdom of Israel, the Queen of Sheba was disappointed about the stories she had been told regarding the great King Solomon. However, her disappointment was not because what she heard was untrue, and it wasn't because she was lied to, either. Let me further explain. History reports the following about the Queen of Sheba's experience:

> So [King] Solomon answered all [the queen of Sheba's] questions; nothing was too difficult for the king [Solomon] to explain to her. When the queen of Sheba observed [the glory of] all of Solomon's wisdom, the palace he had built, the food at his table, his servants' residence, his attendants' service and their attire, his cupbearers, and the burnt offerings he offered at the Lord's temple, it took her breath away.
>
> She said to the king, "The report I heard in my own country about your words and about your wisdom is true. But I didn't believe the report until I came and saw it with my own eyes. **Indeed, I was not even told half.** Your wisdom and prosperity far exceed the report I heard." (emphasis mine)[20]

---

20 1 Kings 10:3-7 (Holman Christian Standard Bible)

The Queen of Sheba felt deceived because she believed "I was not even told half"! What she had heard was true, but it wasn't the *whole* truth! The other half was not told!

Your life has a compelling and undeniable story that is not easily told in its entirety. Friends and family, colleagues, and countrymen may think they have heard all about your story; however, they will be wrong. They may *think* they've seen it all, and they will still be wrong. Unless you open up and share your story—the greatest story ever told—many will never realize that the other half was not told!

Every person has a story. *You* have a story. The world is disadvantaged and incomplete without your story. So, I urge you to tell your story—for the benefit of humanity!

Tell your story because...

1. **Those who tell their stories speak their truth.**
    You've heard it said that there are two sides to every story. The world has heard the story of others about you. The other half is yet to be told. You have "the other side" of that story. Speak your truth.

2. **Those who tell their stories change the conversation.**
    Many great ideas started as a conversation. Unless you share your story, the world will keep telling its own story. If you want to change the conversation, you must tell your story.

3. **Those who tell their stories change the world.**
    Plato, the ancient Greek philosopher, once said, "Those who tell stories rule society." How true!

You *owe humanity* a great story. *The longer your silence, the greater the violence.* Your story brings hope. Your story inspires other dreams. To be silent is to be violent! To be silent is to rob humanity of the awesomeness that you represent. Claim your turn at the microphone of life and speak.